# TALES FROM THE VICARAGE

# TALES FROM THE VICARAGE

## Volume III

## THE INTERVIEWS

by Lionel Birnie & Adam Leventhal

PELOTON PUBLISHING
www.pelotonpublishing.co.uk

First published in Great Britain in 2014
by Peloton Publishing

Typeset by Peloton Publishing
Printed and bound by SS Media

ISBN 978-0-9567814-9-9

Peloton Publishing Ltd
2 Gaddesden Lane, Redbourn, St Albans, AL3 7NP
Registered company number: 7353619

www.lionelbirnie.com
www.pelotonpublishing.co.uk
info@lionelbirnie.com

Jacket photograph: Richard Heathcote / Getty Images

# TALES FROM THE VICARAGE

## CONTENTS

**Lionel Birnie** is a journalist, author and Watford fan. He has written and edited five books about the Hornets. *Four Seasons* is a glossy, hardback book featuring photographs by Alan Cozzi and telling the story of Graham Taylor's second spell as Watford manager between 1997 and 2001. Lionel then wrote *Enjoy the Game*, which documents Watford's incredible rise from the Fourth Division to the top flight and the FA Cup final, based on exclusive interviews with the players and management, and *The 100 Greatest Watford Wins*. In 2012, he started the *Tales from the Vicarage* series. He also covers cycling for *The Sunday Times* and is co-host of The Telegraph Cycling Podcast and co-editor of *The Cycling Anthology*.

**Adam Leventhal** is a TV presenter, journalist and author. He wrote chapters for the first two volumes of *Tales from the Vicarage*. In the first, he spoke to two previous Watford managers, Brendan Rodgers and Malky Mackay, on the topic of loyalty, in the second he interviewed the club's leading goalscorer Luther Blissett and other significant marksmen about the art of scoring goals.

The lifelong Hornet, a veteran of the family terrace, hosted the sold-out Tales from the Vicarage Live event at Watford Palace Theatre that featured Blissett, Sean Dyche and Aidy Boothroyd.

His career in broadcasting started at Capital Radio Sport in London in 1995 before he moved to Sky Sports News in 2003. For two decades he has reported and presented from key sporting fixtures and tournaments around the world including controversial cricket tours and news events.

# INTRODUCTION

## BY THE EDITOR

Every player who has pulled on a Watford shirt and every manager who has ever taken his seat on the bench has a story to tell. Whether their time at Vicarage Road represents the pinnacle of their career, or a point on their journey towards greater things, whether their stay was lengthy or fleeting, a part of their lives will always be golden.

For this, the third volume in the *Tales from the Vicarage* series, Adam Leventhal and I wanted to talk to 11 people who have played a significant part in the Hornets' recent history.

Between them, the people interviewed in this book have played more than 1,000 games for Watford, managed more than 300 matches and scored almost 200 goals. They have won promotion, battled relegation and taken the team on some glorious cup runs.

Their stories span the past 30 years and, as you will see, some of them are interconnected, further proving the point that history is a tapestry of events rather than a straight line.

We hope you enjoy the collection of interviews we have put together and that each story sparks your own memories.

There are a few people we'd like to thank for their help in producing the book, particularly Sam Jackson, Claire Draycott, Ryan Mann, Ellis Bacon and Sam Suresh.

**Lionel Birnie**

# SEAN DYCHE

**On his season as manager**
'I'm not trying to make out everything was rosy. I'm just trying to say that there were some good things going on. Was the boardroom a happy, healthy place? Probably not. But I was quite happy sorting the team out, winning games, doing my best for the club and for the fans.'

# 1

Watch Sean Dyche on the touchline and it's easy to sum up his character as a football manager who shouts, screams and rules by fear. Isn't it?

When the Pozzos took over in 2012, their first act was to relieve Dyche of his managerial duties after one over-achieving season in charge.

Few would have predicted then that Dyche would make it to the Premier League before the Hornets, but he did.

Perhaps Dyche really was the one that got away?

Think you know him? Read on, and be prepared to think again.

# SEAN DYCHE

It didn't have to be a particularly quiet night at Vicarage Road for you to hear Sean Dyche's rasping voice as he bellowed instructions to his players from the invisible cage that prevents managers from getting too close. He has a voice straight from the military parade ground – that of a fearsome drill instructor you definitely wouldn't want to cross.

He's got an army sergeant's hair cut too. And what about that fiery red hair? He's going to have a temper, isn't he? He looks, and sounds, like an angry man.

If you were judging Sean Dyche on first impressions you might come to that conclusion, but he's a far more complex and compelling character than meets the eye. He can raise his voice and show his temper, sure, but he's also thoughtful, quick-witted and funny.

## THE MAN

That voice, then. He's got to be a smoker of, what, 30, 40 a day? Okay, if not a smoker, definitely a shouter, a bawler.

It's a very distinctive voice but does he mind talking about it? Will it touch a nerve? Sitting down opposite Dyche might be intimidating if you judged him on his appearance, his voice, which is several notes below gruff, and his reputation as a no-nonsense centre half and uncompromising manager. But the key to understanding Sean Dyche is not to fear the exterior, just ask the questions.

Basically, he's a nice bloke and not one to get upset as long as you are fair. He's a fan of an analogy, as you will see, so he won't mind this one. He's like an onion. He's multi-layered and although he may have the power to make you cry, that's not his main objective.

So, back to the voice. When did it become as rough as sandpaper? Apparently, it runs in the family – on the male side, at least – and he had a deep voice from a young age.

Like me, you are probably picturing a small ginger boy with grown-up Sean Dyche's voice, which creates quite an amusing image. 'It was a slightly lighter version of it but always with that gruffness,' he says.

On a more serious note, I wondered if he has had it checked out to make sure there's not a problem with his throat. He has, and there isn't, which is a relief. 'I've had people say all sorts. My favourite was when I was at Watford and they used to say "exhaust pipe throat", as if I smoked an exhaust pipe before I went out in the morning.'

There were others too. They said he had the perfect voice for an adult chatline, or that he'd chewed a bag of gravel.

But the voice suits the job of a football manager. 'It's good and bad, yin and yang,' he says. 'If I change my tone it doesn't sound authentic, so I just attempt to be like this all the time, good or bad.

'If I try to be like "Hey!"' he says in a higher tone, 'or immediately jolly, they'll go, "Oh that's bizarre – what's all that about?"'

There was one occasion when Dyche tried to break the mould on a League Managers Association course. The experience taught him a valuable lesson.

'They said, "We want you to share a story," so I started talking in this high pitched voice and they said, "Oh, that doesn't suit anything about you, your persona, your look. None of that suits." They said: "Look, you've got to be authentic, because if not, they [the players] will smell bullshit.'"

So Dyche has never tried to be something he's not but he's well aware that after his departure from Watford, which we will discuss later, he needed to show the wider world that he had more strings to his bow. He might have been in danger of being type-cast. The voice, the appearance, his career as a tough-tackling British defender for less-than-glamorous clubs all might easily have restricted his opportunities in a game that is ready to pigeon-hole people.

'One of the things that actually did me a world of good was doing some work for Sky Sports,' he explains. 'People thought there's more to him than the drill instructor. I reckon they thought, "I bet he runs them hard and he's a mean old fashioned football manager," but through doing games as a pundit people thought, "Hang on a minute – he's got some half decent views."'

It's an honest assessment from a man who knew he had to put himself in the shop window as a man and a manager as well as be prepared to change people's perceptions of him.

'People thought I obviously like a bit of a laugh, which I do, but I think about things way more deeply than people think I do because I'm educated.' Then the appraisal reaches the crux of the matter. 'People think, "Who is this tyrant?" It's the biggest misconception about me. Over the last couple of years that's changed, but if you ask the players they'll say, "Does he shout? No." I've got it in me, but it's not something I do every day, or every week. I'd rather go for educating rather than shouting every day of the week.'

But just as he's keen to force people to look deeper than the surface when assessing him, so he likes to use his own perceptiveness to learn about others, particularly the players he works with.

'I've watched footballers all through my life,' he says. 'They'll say to me, "Boss, how do you always know what's going on?"'

'Because I've watched thousands of players. I watch their body language, twists, turns, highs, lows, head up, head back, shoulders back, all of it.

– What's wrong with you? I'll say.
– Nothing, they'll say.
– Yes there is, I can tell. What's up?
– Oh, I've just got a bit of a cold.
– No problem. Just get yourself to the doc.'

Dyche as the quiet, caring, nurturing coach doesn't quite fit the stereotype of a man who seems to attract the attention of the cameras when he's yelling from the touchline but, whisper it quietly, he does have a softer side.

* * *

You may not have heard of Sean Dyche's love of shoes.

'It's not Imelda Marcos love,' he says quickly to clarify any misconception. 'I haven't got 400 pairs.'

He opens the cupboard under the stairs to reveal an array of footwear. He's rifling through pair after pair. There are some Patrick Cox boots – 'designer flavour from back in the day' – and a pair to suit every occasion. Then he explains the intricacies of Prada's takeover of Church's which, he says, was a significant move in the shoe industry.

'My real collection is upstairs,' he says, leading the way.

As we approach the stairs, I ask if I should take off my shoes. Knowing that a man is often judged by his shoes, I had chosen a decent pair specially.

I ask Dyche for his verdict, which is fairly damning.

'They're glued,' he says, referring, I assume, to the soles.

'But no need to take them off,' he adds as we head upstairs.

'The kids have done all sorts on the carpet.'

We step into the walk-in wardrobe in the bedroom and he reveals he has several pairs of shoes that are the same design but each have a different type of sole to suit the conditions. This is the sort of attention to detail I hadn't realised existed in the footwear world, although it does, perhaps, explain why Dyche has not slipped over on the touchline, as Beppe Sannino did on one occasion, despite getting fairly animated at times.

And so it should come as no surprise to find that Dyche has special shoes for matchdays.

'These are Jeffrey West,' he says, holding a pair out like a salesman who knows the customer can't afford to touch. 'The real top end of the market,' he says proudly before showing another pair with rubber soles. 'They're waterproof. Real leather soles go like mush.

'Look at these,' he says showing a pair that looks, to me, identical to the last. 'Stitched sole, high-quality handmade shoes.

'A lovely chestnut colour, these ones,' he says, moving on. 'These are original Barkers.... These are a shaped-toe brogue.'

His passion, like his knowledge, is impressive and it turns out his shoe fetish, like his voice, is genetic.

'My mum worked in shoes,' he tells me. 'She'd stitch them and make the lasts.' At that moment I assume Dyche had meant to say, 'She'd stitch them to make them *last*,' but I don't correct him. Later I learn that he meant what he said and that 'lasts' are a key component in shoe-making.

I ask what it is about shoes that fascinates him. 'It's a love of the craft. I very rarely buy any poor kinds of footwear,' he says. At that point, I instinctively look down at my feet and my 'glued' soles and shudder, which I sense he notices.

There's something about Dyche's interest in good quality footwear that seems entirely appropriate. Our feet are our contact with the world. He's into solid foundations, and a sense of remaining grounded. A long career in football has not given him airs and graces. As regularly as he can, he goes for an Indian meal with a group of what he describes as 'hardcore' friends – mates he's known since he was five years old.

There's no opportunity to get carried away just because he's preparing his team to face Chelsea or Manchester United at the weekend.

'They know me, warts and all, the ins and outs, the ups and downs, the good times and bad, and they don't bother me about football even though one of them actually works as a scout for Everton,' he says. 'We basically just tell the same stories a thousand times over. The fish we caught gets a bit bigger, the woman gets a bit prettier or uglier, whichever way the story goes. They probably don't know how important those nights are to me.'

They're important because Dyche consciously aims to keep his work and his life balanced. He's acutely aware that switching off when he's away from football is important.

'Some people go on about loving football, so they get home and watch football endlessly. I don't. It's not my thing,' he admits. 'I like to be fresh to do what I do the next day. When I get home, obviously I have to do the usual stuff like phone calls and watch key games, but my life is not obsessed with football.'

The proof of this can be found walking around Dyche's house, which is on a golfing estate in Northamptonshire. Its location would be a persuasive red herring in an episode of *Through the Keyhole* – lots of footballers love golf – but there are no clues to Dyche's career to be found. There aren't any photos or memorabilia on the walls, no framed shirts or trophies. It turns out that's a deliberate decision. He doesn't want any part of his house becoming a Sean Dyche shrine.

'I've never had anything in any of my houses,' says Dyche. 'At Chesterfield, I had a house with about three wardrobes, a couple of beds and that was virtually it, partly because I wasn't getting paid a king's ransom,' he says. 'Then I moved to Bristol City and bought a nice house, but it wasn't really my bag to start loading it full of football gear. I don't want to keep reminding myself, good or bad, every day when I'm walking around my house.

'I don't need a photo to remind me of good times. I've got it locked within me, so I know how it feels.'

Dyche accepts it's a personal choice, and he has friends in the game who live in houses that are like mini museums to their own careers, but he chooses to prioritise other things.

'It can get dominating for your partner, I think. I've never really spoken to my family about it but I could imagine there being a feeling of, "Oh, yet more stuff to fill the house."

'Then kids come along and I don't want their lives or my wife's life to be all about me. It's their life too. We share a life and they have their own so they don't want their home full of my stuff. I understand if people have a specific room for their football stuff but even that would be too much for me. I don't know; it's just not part of my personality.'

Perhaps having a house that shows no signs of his day job eases the pressure because he admits he wouldn't be human if he didn't take his work home with him sometimes. He says he's good at 'compartmentalising it' and he tries to prevent football from seeping into every aspect of his life, particularly if he's getting a hard time in the press, although he can't stop his family reading the papers.

'My dad still believes the papers more than he believes me. I'll tell him we played really well and he'll say, "Oh, well it didn't say that in the paper." I think: "So, you believe the paper and not your son, who's the manager?" Very strange.'

## THE PLAYER

Having steered Burnley to promotion from the Championship, Dyche has now managed in England's top division, although he never played there. During his 19-season career, he spent almost three-quarters of his time in the lower divisions. Although he doesn't have them on display in a cabinet, Dyche does have four promotion-winning medals tucked away from his time with Chesterfield, Bristol City, Millwall and Northampton. His last taste of success as a player came with the Cobblers in 2006, helping them out of League Two a year after he left Watford, in what turned out to be the penultimate season as a player.

Dyche started his career at Nottingham Forest under Brian Clough. He may not have made a first-team appearance for them but he does do a decent Cloughie impression. He joined Chesterfield and almost captained them to the FA Cup final in 1997 after scoring the penalty to put them 2-0 up against Middlesbrough at Old Trafford, only for Ravanelli and Juninho to inspire a comeback. Chesterfield lost the replay. Dyche moved on to Bristol City and then Millwall before Ray Lewington brought him to Vicarage Road on a free transfer in 2002. Lewington was rebuilding the team on a drastically reduced budget after the excesses of Gianluca Vialli's year in charge and Dyche's uncomplicated approach to defending offered stability where previously there had been flakiness.

No sooner had Dyche arrived than the squad was plunged into the chill of financial uncertainty when they were asked to take a 12 per cent wage deferral. The move to help the club avoid administration made sense, even if it left Dyche scratching his head. 'The biggest twist in it for me was that I'd only signed six weeks earlier so I said, "Why didn't you just give me 12 per cent less?"' he says. 'I was confused. They'd just given it to me and now they were taking it away? It was a bit surreal.'

Despite his confusion, he was an advocate of the move, and the players agreed, collectively, to the temporary cut. 'It was a considered decision from a good group of players,' Dyche says. 'Some of the older players, who had a bit more money, took more of a cut, and the younger players took less, while anyone below a certain wage didn't lose out at all.'

It wasn't the last time he found himself working in dire financial circumstances – although things didn't get quite as bad when he was the Watford manager – and in adversity came a greater feeling of togetherness. Being up against it created a siege mentality that the players capitalised on.

Although he'd only been at the club a few weeks when the proposal to reduce the wages was made, Dyche found himself bringing the group together.

'It was a strange time, but weirdly positive, because it did mould the dynamic of the group. I said, "We've gotta turn this into a positive and spin this for the club in a good way. If we don't take the cut, the club will be in a bit of a state, which doesn't help any of us."'

As a natural leader, Dyche captained the team later in the season, although he was unceremoniously sent off in his first match as skipper, in a 1-0 home defeat against Preston North End. The suspension that followed disrupted the end of the season for him and he was an unused sub in the FA Cup semi-final defeat to Southampton at Villa Park.

His 'middle season', as he describes it, included two matches that he deems his most memorable while at the club. The first came at the turn of the new year – FA Cup third-round day – when Chelsea were in town for a 21,000 capacity sell-out. The financial muscle of the two clubs couldn't have been more different after Roman Abramovich had plumbed his monetary pipeline in at Stamford Bridge, but the cash-strapped Hornets dug in that day. For Dyche, it came out of the blue, and he found himself up against a Chelsea strikeforce of Eidur Gudjohnsen and Adrian Mutu.

'I hadn't played in quite a few weeks and Neil Cox was suspended. It's not easy going into a game like that when you haven't been playing, trust me,' he says.

Watford exceeded expectations and boosted their own coffers by holding the millionaires to a 2-2 draw to earn a replay. All the goals came in the first half with Watford leading twice before being pegged back on both occasions. It made for a second half of hard graft and, subsequently, delight for the centre back.

'It was on TV, it was tough and I hadn't played in ages, so I was weirdly... proud of myself,' Dyche eventually concedes.

Watford lost the replay at Stamford Bridge 4-0, but two months later they had more pressing concerns. Three defeats in a row had left them two places off the relegation zone and in desperate need of three points. Derby were in the mire too, so it was a case of dog eat dog when the two sides met under lights at Vicarage Road. It was a night Dyche still holds very close to his heart. After Derby took an early lead, Watford fought back to win 2-1.

'I'd come back into the team and it was massive – a really important game,' Dyche bristles, as if he's giving a pre-match team talk. 'Gavin Mahon scored the winner and I was very good on that night. I'm not just saying that but I was. It was a big performance in a big game.'

The following season would be his last for Watford. There were highs with the League Cup wins over Southampton and Portsmouth, both of which Dyche played in, but his season ended prematurely when he was injured in the New Year's Day victory against his old club, Millwall.

He would never wear a Watford shirt again. Once Aidy Boothroyd, Lewington's replacement, had steered Watford to safety, Dyche found himself surplus to requirements. Perhaps Dyche was also a little too outspoken for the rookie manager.

'I knew it was coming and I knew he [Aidy] wanted his own version of me, which was Malky Mackay,' he says.

Dyche suspected Boothroyd had doubts about letting an experienced, respected defender go, and he was right. He put his manager's decision to the test.

'We had this final meeting and I said, "Come on, tell me the truth." He said, "I've made a bad decision here." He said he thought I should be staying and he realised that although I could be quite opinionated and full-on, I meant well. But I said: "No, it's done now. We've got to part."'

Maybe that decision weighed on Boothroyd and perhaps he realised what he was missing once Dyche's voice could no longer be heard around the place because, before long, Dyche was back at Vicarage Road.

## THE COACH

After a couple of seasons at Northampton, now aged 36, Dyche hung up his boots and fixed his sights on a coaching career. His first job was at Watford, as part of the youth system.

'Fair play to him,' Dyche says of Boothroyd. 'Of course he remembered how he let me go, but when I wanted to become a coach he employed me and I've always admired him for that.'

Dyche, a fan of learning from experience, clearly appreciated that his former manager had done that very thing. 'Most managers would not do that. He'd seen beyond the player I was and saw the person I was, I think. He'd not really spoken to me in depth as a player but I think he'd thought, "He's a good type, let's get him in."'

Dyche took up the role of youth team coach in August 2007. He says that from the age of 26 he knew he wanted to go into coaching when his playing days were over, and he spent the final decade of his career observing his own managers and coaches.

'I was looking at Aidy Boothroyd, Ray Lewington, Ray Harford, Mark McGhee, who worked with Harford at Millwall, and John Duncan at Chesterfield, a coach-style manager, so I knew quite early that this was for me somewhere down the line,' he says.

There are two more names that also helped shape Dyche's next step: Swassing and Barbe. As you wrack your brains trying to place them as assistant managers or kit men at Watford, Millwall or Chesterfield, I have to tell you that neither of them have anything to do with football, as far as I am aware.

This is where we take an unexpected turn into something resembling a paragraph that might have appeared in a textbook at school.

Swassing and Barbe, or Raymond Swassing and Walter Barbe to give them their full names, are actually academics who are notable for devising the Swassing-Barbe Modality Index, which focuses on how individuals learn and process information. The theory is that almost anything can be learned through visual, audio and kinaesthetic (or tactile) means. To put that into simple terms, you learn by watching, listening or doing.

Dyche found that when he made the switch from playing to coaching, he had to make the shift from receiving information to giving it. This, he says, has its difficulties.

'When you're a player, you're in a suit of armour. You have to be invincible, so you get into defence mode pretty quickly,' says Dyche.

Football is a game in which mistakes are common. It's also a macho environment and not always a sympathetic one. Often the spotlight of blame bounces around the dressing room until it concentrates its beam on the weakest by default.

Sometimes it can be an environment that makes constructive learning difficult.

As Dyche explains: 'A manager will say, "Why did you do that?" and the response will be, "Well, why not?" So when you're a coach or manager, you have to accept that when you offer information to someone, they're probably going to be in defensive mode.'

His challenge was to be able to soften barriers that he had probably been putting up himself not long before as a player, to ensure his message was getting across to those who were now under his charge.

'Even now I try to tick the boxes with our group with the VAKWD model: visual, audio, kinaesthetic, written and discussion. We'll find a way of floating your boat with information,' he says, almost as if it's a catchphrase.

However, as has always been the case, convincing players that your way is the right way takes time, as Dyche explains.

'At first they're there and you're there and there's a kind of posturing, like in fencing,' he says, drawing the battle lines with his hands. 'You're waiting, tapping each other's sword, and then eventually you get a bit closer and contact is made. Then at the end of the match you've got to decide whether you're both gonna walk away with a "well played" or if you're going to get stabbed,' he says bluntly.

This tentative jousting between a coach and his players may seem like a strange analogy, but it highlights how difficult it can be for a recently-retired player to get his message across to his team.

And his talk about modality indices, rather than teacups thrown or hairdryers blown, indicates how coaching methods have changed. The emphasis now is more on teaching than instructing, on improving rather than blaming.

'Back in the day you'd get, "What did you do that for?" from a manager. Immediately the hackles are up and the armour goes on. But this is about us moving forward, not about us saying, "See, I told you that was wrong!" This is about us asking, "Are you aware of it, do you understand it, can we change it, that's why, that's what I learned and that's what I mean,'" he says, his tone softening with every word.

Being able to tell players what they are doing wrong without demoralising them, helping them to improve without developing a fear of failure, is a skill. Dyche becomes defensive when I ask whether relatively complex arguments might be wasted on the average footballer.

'Yet again that's a misconception. It's a perception, not a fact,' he says. 'There are some players I deal with who are very bright. If you want brutal, I can give you brutal and it's bang, bang, bang, okay let's go. But there are players who want more detail. One isn't a better approach than the other, it's just the way they want information. The key is to offer it in the style they want it.'

Dyche became closer to Boothroyd as a coach than he had been as a player and as Watford's first season back in the Championship tailed off dramatically, he found he had to give the boss some home truths.

'One day he said, "Does anyone think I've gone soft?" Everyone went deathly quiet. I said, "I do." I had to be honest with him. Everyone was reflecting on him getting too precise with everything, but it actually went the other way: you had players who were beginning to get it all done for them and it was too much, too good, and the players began to get soft as well.'

When Boothroyd left, Dyche assisted Malky Mackay, who stood in as caretaker manager before Brendan Rodgers was appointed and then took up a role with the Academy.

Rodgers had arrived from the Chelsea Academy and had

very clear ideas about how training should be conducted.

'He had these ultra-detailed session plans,' explains Dyche. 'But he never thought, "I'm now at Watford so I'll have to be flexible here." I was thinking, "Oh my God, how am I going to do this?"

'In the end, I had to say: "Gaffer, I need to give you an idea of my role here. I get up at six in the morning, drive past the training ground, get the van, pick up the team at Watford, take them back to the training ground, make sure the kit is washed, then plan the session, go out, deliver the session on my own, have lunch, go out and deliver the second session, do their education lessons with them, get back on the bus, drive them back to Watford, then drive back to the office to do the admin work, then go to Harefield School in the evening to do another coaching session, leave that and go and watch the first team... The chance of me getting an hour to do one of those sessions bang on is very, very unlikely."'

Dyche takes a deep breath.

'Bren had this funny manner, but he was very good with it.' He impersonates Rodgers with a near-perfect Northern Irish accent, albeit a bit gruffer. 'Aye, aye, good, right there. I'll leave that with you then.'

'I was wondering what that meant. Do I try to do the sessions or not do 'em? I thought, "well, I'll just crack on."'

It was a difficult start to a relationship that has blossomed as both men have risen to the Premier League – Rodgers with Swansea and Liverpool, Dyche at Burnley.

And Dyche believes Rodgers' few months at Watford were a fast-track learning experience for him. 'It was interesting to see someone come out of Chelsea fighting for acceptance because no one really knew him. The Chelsea badge is a strong one, so sometimes it was like he was saying, "Look I was at Chelsea, I know what I'm doing." Now he doesn't need to tell you he knows what he's doing, he's a lot more at ease.'

Rodgers certainly didn't shy away from trying to implement his own style of play either. Dyche sums up how the players, staff and fans felt about the sudden, jolting transition from Boothroyd's style to Rodgers. It was a case of trying to take the team from one extreme to the other overnight.

'Everyone was thinking, "What's going on here?"' he says, before recalling the defining moment that summed up Rodgers' early days at Vicarage Road. 'Liam Bridcutt got a free-kick in the centre circle and he passed it back to the keeper. The Watford fans went mental. It was like, "What are you doing?"'

'It was too much,' Dyche says, before explaining that Rodgers 'flexed his philosophy'.

We had more mixed football. Play the pass if you want to, go long if you have to, and by the end he was doing it very well.'

At the end of the season, Rodgers left, controversially, to join Reading. It's a move he discusses at length in volume one of the *Tales from the Vicarage* series, and it was a move that gave Dyche another opportunity.

Malky Mackay, the man who had taken Dyche's place in the Watford team, was now the permanent manager and Dyche was his assistant. They made a formidable pair on the touchline until Mackay decided to join Cardiff in the summer of 2011. Mackay wanted to take Dyche with him but the move to Wales didn't appeal. Besides, he was ready to take his next big leap.

## THE MANAGER

At this point of the interview, just as we were preparing to talk about Dyche's sometimes turbulent season as Watford manager, he is in the middle of uttering the words, 'I knew what the script was...' when the doorbell interrupts us.

It couldn't have been a more symbolic moment had it been

Laurence Bassini at the door. In fact, it was Dyche's wife, who had just come back from the shops and needed a hand with some bags.

When we pick up the conversation, Dyche explains why he didn't follow Malky to Cardiff, opting to stay at Watford where the budget would be tight and the opportunities to mould a team limited.

'There were a load of different reasons why I didn't: family, I live 50 miles away, their contract didn't suit me and it was my chance to be manager, which was a great opportunity.'

Having seen Mackay promoted after Rodgers left, Dyche felt he had a good chance of getting the job.

'I'd always been formulating my ideas about management and learning all the time,' he says. 'It was a Championship club, I liked the environment, the people, the structures, I knew it all like the back of my hand and I knew all the challenges. I knew the not-so-good side of it, so I wasn't exactly naïve; I wasn't going into it with my eyes closed.'

Dyche believed the club was in 'reasonable shape' when he took over. There were, he said, 'assets on the football pitch and a few young players who needed time', but Danny Graham, Don Cowie and Will Buckley had departed, leaving the team short of firepower and creativity. 'Well, that was 54 per cent of the previous season's goals gone,' he says. 'And the budget was lower than the year before too.'

In January, Marvin Sordell would follow them as Watford lived up to their reputation as a selling club. But Dyche was not labouring under false pretences.

'I was told, "Right, Sean, this is what's gonna happen. You're gonna lose him, lose him and lose him and the amount you have to spend is that,"' he says with a wry smile.

Dyche wasn't daunted. 'I'd had a weird experience with Watford. I went there as a player when the money had gone. I'd basically signed for Ramon Vega's tax bill – that's what I was earning – so I'd never known any of that kind of funding. The year they went to the Premier League, I wasn't there, and when I came back into the youth department, with all due respect, there's not the funding like the first team, so I'd never really known the club to have any money.'

Dyche's reign started with a poor run: only ten points were collected from the first 13 matches, including seven defeats. Then came the dramatic turnaround. Watford lost only seven of their next 33 games and rose to 11th in the table – higher than either Mackay or Rodgers had finished.

He'd exceeded expectations by quite some distance, 'with a group that was written off after 13 games as being a horrible group,' he recalls. 'People probably thought we were really poor without even thinking. Then they realised, "Wow, actually there are some pretty good players here."'

The pride of his achievement in turning around fortunes still shines through. 'I don't think that's bad,' he says under-statedly before carrying on. 'It shows clear statistical signs of development, so that was the thing I really enjoyed about my one season as manager of Watford. Bottom four club in terms of wage bill, finished 11th, highest finish in four seasons – trust me, it's a really hard thing to do.'

So the money was tight and from the outside looking in it seemed that working under owner Laurence Bassini was tough. Stories of boardroom unrest centring on the controversial owner never seemed far away.

'All I would say is that Laurence was always all right with me and the football staff. I've got no baggage about Laurence at all because anything that was allegedly going on was separate from me,' says Dyche. 'I never witnessed anything that was bizarre at board level.'

Dyche credits Bassini with not interfering in football

matters too. 'He knew he didn't know as much as me or the staff about football, so he wasn't remotely trying to tell me anything about football, and that was really where our paths would've crossed,' he outlines. 'Some owners do suddenly grow an opinion about football and start asking the manager, "Why aren't we doing this, that and the other?" but he didn't do that.'

Obviously Dyche was aware that Mackay's relationship with the owner had broken down prior to his departure. However, the new manager was keen to take the rough with the smooth and get on with his first managerial job.

'I was willing to work within the confinements, the restrictions, the parameters,' he says. 'I was quite happy with it or I wouldn't have done the job. I knew it was gonna be tough and I knew there were many people thinking, "No – don't give it to him; we want a big name," like all fans do,' he says defiantly. 'I also knew what I was doing. I knew I could do it, knew I could bring in the people to help me do it, bring in the players to help and develop those players.'

Dyche does concede that Bassini did have different sides to his personality but says: 'My relationship with him was pretty normal – nothing like how he got himself involved with the press. There was none of that going on with us on the football side. There was never any ranting or raving about this or that,' he says as I reflect on some of my dealings with Bassini at the time, before refocussing on the job at hand.

'I'm not trying to make out that everything was rosy,' he says. 'I'm just trying to say that there were some good things going on. Was the boardroom a happy, healthy place? Probably not. Did I have to be in that boardroom very often? No. Was I party to it? No. Did I need or want to be party to it? No. I was quite happy sorting the team out, winning games, getting players developed, doing my best for the club and for the fans.'

Dyche said earlier that he has the ability to 'lock things

within', and it's at a moment like this that you get a crystal-clear view into what he means when he says that. He doesn't want people to rewrite history.

'There were an awful lot of good things. Opinion changes because of the name of a bloke who owned it, but if you think about it rationally, forget the bloke who owned it and popular opinion at the time,' he says as he prepares to once again reel off a persuasive argument to back up his claim.

'We had a low wage bill, good structuring through all departments – youth team, development squad and first team squad – good analysts, good office staff, good support staff, good processes, good protocol, good organisation, good links with the community...' He pauses, changes gear and goes again. 'I'm just trying to bring balance to the story. It all got a bit negative but you've got to see beyond that. Trust me – I was on the inside.'

As if there wasn't enough going on at the time – including the imminent takeover by the Pozzos, which ultimately proved to be the end for Dyche, and which we'll come to – one of the assets that was plying his trade at the club was soon to be at the centre of controversy: Troy Deeney's imprisonment for affray occurred on the rookie manager's watch too.

Dyche admits that the full gravity of the crime, which took place in Birmingham in February 2012, only really became clear to him about ten weeks afterwards. 'Troy had been quite casual about telling me the depth of the incident,' he reveals. 'Then, of course, more facts came to light and lawyers started speaking to the club.'

The manager knew that this wasn't a 'smack-on-the-wrist type situation' as he described it, but was keen to maintain a consistent line from the very start. That position was to support his player unequivocally.

'I made it quite clear in my opinion that in no circumstances should he be removed from the club. I said we're a club that believes in development. People develop in different ways, people have different challenges.' Dyche was well aware that it had the potential to be a contentious position. 'Many supporters had said that they wanted him out. I said absolutely not – in my opinion, absolutely not.'

The line had been drawn by Dyche, and he had his reasons.

'The courts talk about rehab, education, so why shouldn't we? I thought, "He has made a mistake but I don't think he's a bad person." You pay the price, and we just try to educate along the way. You've got to give people a chance to change.'

Dyche believed in the individuals he worked with to respond to adversity in a positive way and to learn from their mistakes. That was what he was trying to instil in the players on the football pitch, so why couldn't it apply to everyday life too?

Dyche was Watford's manager when Deeney started his jail term but was no longer in charge when the striker came out.

## THE EX-MANAGER

It's time for a break before we conclude this journey. Put the kettle on, grind the coffee beans – yes, grind the beans – because Dyche wants a hot drink. Won't instant coffee do? No, it certainly won't where he is concerned.

'You're a coffee snob, aren't you?' I ask.

'Oh definitely a coffee snob – I don't like instant coffee. It has to be real coffee,' he insists.

It might simply be a coincidence that Dyche is happy to put a little more time and effort into something that he enjoys, like brewing the perfect cup of coffee, but I suspect it isn't. It's something that extends out of the kitchen and into his work as a football manager. Good things come to those who wait, you might say. Over to Sean to join the dots from analogy to reality.

'Just-add-water management is impossible. Everyone wants it yesterday, everyone wants it in an instant, everyone wants it now,' he says. 'As a manager, rationally, it just doesn't happen like that, or rarely it happens like that.'

Dyche had sewn seeds in the 2011-12 season, yet his organic arable plot was soon to be ploughed and replanted with a continental crop courtesy of the Pozzo takeover. The long-range forecast had predicted climactic change at the club from the turn of the year.

'First there were rumours that it might happen, but it didn't, then there were rumblings that it might happen again, but it was delayed, and then it did happen and it literally went like that,' he says with a click of his fingers.

The winds of change blew away the clouds of uncertainty that had hung over Dyche and Vicarage Road. It was clear quite early on that he would not be the man for the Pozzos.

'I've been in football since I was 16, and it's fair to say it came to me pretty quick about the probability versus the possibility of me going,' he says. 'I conducted myself in the right manner because the club is more important than me.'

Typically, Dyche went about his business in 'the right fash-ion' as he recalls. His last involvement with the players was to kick-start their pre-season training schedule with a three-day session to 'check them out' before a further two-week break.

With Gianfranco Zola waiting in the wings, Dyche was told at the start of July that his services would no longer be required. It won't surprise you to hear that the man who went on to lead Burnley to the Premier League two seasons later, while saying there were a 'few interesting twists and turns', doesn't look back in anger.

'It happens. Companies get bought out, companies change, managers get moved, managers get shipped out, managers get made redundant,' he says. 'People are in a lot worse state than me, by the way, so I'm not going to cry about it. That's football, you can lose your job for almost any reason. It's just more brutal because it's public, it's in your face, it's written about, there's endless opinion about it. But this sort of stuff goes on every day.'

Dyche acknowledges the fact that he was a victim of circumstance by stating, 'I just didn't fit the model,' but he's not feeling sorry for himself, and the feeling was mutual.

'They made a good decision because it wouldn't have worked. Not because I'm not good at doing what I do, but it wouldn't have worked: it's a different model, it's a European style model,' he says. 'The owner and technical director have a big say in everything that goes on – not just the business side, but the football side.'

In the same way that he aims to empower players to get on with their jobs, Dyche expected and received the same treatment as a manager from those above him while at Watford.

'Aidy made it clear when I was youth team boss that I could do what I want, and when I took over as manager, Graham Taylor [who was chairman], said, "By the way Sean, you'll get nothing from me. It's your job. If you want me, I'm there for you, but it's your job." He was never down the training ground, never putting his tuppence-worth in. He left it to me to take the decisions,' he says.

That's not to say that he and Taylor never spoke. Quite the opposite. The club's most successful manager was a willing on-demand mentor, but not one that was overpowering.

'For him with all his history, particularly all his Watford history, to be so compartmentalised – "This is your job, this is my job," – was brilliant,' Dyche says warmly.

'For a football man to be like that takes a lot of strength. It would have been easy for him to say, "Sean you've got to do it like this, do it like that." So that's why it wouldn't have worked for me with people who want to give their opinion to the manager constantly.'

But what of the bigger picture? The Pozzo model may not have suited Dyche's way of working, but the man who has filled almost every role at Watford says: 'All clubs have to evolve and change. They can't just stay static. You've got to be malleable and flexible to move with the times.' So it can work then? It depends on one key component, according to Dyche.

'Winning solves every problem, and if you're not winning all the time, question marks come, and if you're not winning a lot of the time, then big question marks come,' he says ominously.

So what of the future for Dyche? He's now got 'Premier League manager' written proudly on his CV. He's followed in the footsteps of Mackay and Rodgers who have gone on to have success at clubs after Watford. So how does he deal with the pressure and the trappings of egotism? Both, as you will read elsewhere, snared Boothroyd to some extent as he rose to prominence.

'I'm not still searching for kudos. Aidy had gone from a lower-league player, well thought of as a coach, well thought of in academy circles, to the Premier League and was suddenly rubbing shoulders with big managers,' Dyche explains. 'It was so "through the roof" and a lot to take on.'

It's a topic that Dyche has spoken to his former manager about. 'I understand him, and he's given me some really good advice, and he's very honest about it. Maybe I'll turn out like that but I think I have an innate feel for that kind of stuff, and I'll be surprised if I get ideas above my station.'

Being philosophical about problems that he may encounter is probably a good way of avoiding making the mistake in the future. On that issue, here is an offering to any journalist who intends to speak to Dyche about his 'philosophy'. It's probably best not to. He is not a fan. Listen to this.

'I'll give you a quick snapshot. It drives me mad when we go, "Ah, it's philosophy, it's philosophy, it's philosophy." Oh, get off, will you? At the end of the day, football is about good planning, good preparation and good practice.

'The perception is that if you haven't got "a philosophy" then you're a dullard that hasn't got a clue. That's just not the case. I know it's just a trendy word at the moment but it drives me mad. There are loads of good people doing good things in football and unless you have a philosophy you can almost be deemed an imbecile.'

It seems like we've gone full circle and we're back where we started. Once again we're talking about a misconception. 'I'm not some guru or some future-proof manager because there is no such thing,' Dyche says.

To finish, it's worth reflecting where it all started for him as a footballer in 1987, as a trainee at Nottingham Forest under the stewardship of Brian Clough. He's someone that Dyche is asked about a lot, as it appears some of Clough's managerial magic has rubbed off on him. But that would be too easy, too convenient. 'Fortune favours the prepared,' is one of Dyche's sayings and that gets to the heart of his current success, not his link to a 'mythical character' that he encountered in his teens.

Of course, as Dyche looks back, he realises there are aspects of the way that Clough governed that he has taken with him. 'Simple formats, simple support systems for the group, good discipline, good manners and looking after yourself,' Dyche says clearly to emphasise that over-complicating things will ultimately confuse proceedings.

Two other things that he's keen to talk about when Clough is mentioned, his shoes of course, and a piece of advice that he keeps with him to this day. 'Smile. It costs nothing for a smile.'

It's an expression that sits well with Dyche and completes a picture of a man who has to more to him than meets the eye.

# MICAH HYDE

**On his 'rocking the baby' celebration
against Bolton in April 1999**
'That was for my son, Tyrique.
He's 15 now... You want to
see the size of him.
He's massive, taller than me'

## 2

Micah Hyde and Richard Johnson were the silk and steel in one of the finest midfield partnerships Watford have ever had.

They dovetailed perfectly to drive the Hornets to the Second Division title in 1998, victory at Wembley the following season, and on to the Premiership.

Hyde was a calming presence that balanced Johnson's more aggressive style and they each helped the other raise their game.

Since retiring, Hyde has begun to make his way as a coach and if his passion for the game is anything to go by, he should make it to the top.

# MICAH HYDE

Micah Hyde scored just once during the season Watford were promoted to the Premier League but it's a goal he will remember as long as he lives. The team's bid to make the play-offs had spluttered, choked and seemingly stalled after a run of five games without a win, but a combustible final ten minutes against Tranmere Rovers and victory at Birmingham City on Easter Monday had seen Watford rise from the dead.

On Saturday April 10, 1999, Watford had a home game against Bolton Wanderers. Two days earlier, Hyde's partner had given birth to their first son, Tyrique, and his world had been turned on its head. Twenty-four minutes into the game, Hyde intercepted a loose ball on the edge of the Bolton penalty area and, despite being surrounded by opponents, took a shot at goal. This was not a powerful hit-and-hope effort. It was a deft flick of the boot that steered the ball along a seemingly pre-determined and carefully plotted course past the goalkeeper.

The ball hit the net and Hyde copied the 'cradling the baby' celebration made famous by Brazilian Bebeto during the 1994 World Cup and Nick Wright, Tommy Mooney, Peter Kennedy, Allan Smart, Paul Robinson and Richard Johnson ran to join in.

'Yeah, that was for my son, Tyrique,' Hyde says as we talk in the supporters' bar at Dagenham and Redbridge's Victoria Road ground. 'He's 15 now… 15! It makes you think, doesn't it? I remember that as clear as day, like it was yesterday. You wanna see the size of him. He's massive, taller than me.'

* * *

It's a warm day in June 2014. The World Cup has just got under way and Dagenham's Rainham Road is all white vans, St George's flags and misplaced optimism. The Daggers' stadium is tucked away on a housing estate and retains plenty of its non-league charm, although the team are in League Two these days.

When I arrive, on time, I give Micah Hyde a call. 'You're here already?' he says, with a hint of surprise that does not bode well. 'Give me ten minutes – I've just got to sort the kit out.'

I had heard that Hyde had been a reluctant interviewee during his career – a footballer who preferred to let his feet do the talking. That's a cliché that usually masks a mistrust or dislike of the media.

For 18 months, Hyde had been head of academy coaching at Dagenham and Redbridge but when he arrives in the bar, sauntering casually past the sticky tables and fruit machine, he looks as if he could still be playing. Now 39, he doesn't appear to have aged at all since his Vicarage Road days.

First impressions are that he's polite, but not particularly warm. 'Nice to meet you,' he says. 'How long do you need?'

Before I can answer, he says: 'Will half-an-hour do?'

Ninety minutes later, he's still talking, warmly, humorously, passionately and rapidly. The midfielder who looked so laid back on the pitch actually has a mind and mouth that operate at a hundred miles an hour. Perhaps that's the secret to his game. He thought so quickly that he was able to make his play look effortlessly languid.

Tyrique, his son, is a member of the Dagenham and Redbridge Academy – a teenager dreaming of making it to the Premier League like his dad. Tyrique is a midfielder too, so I wonder if he has inherited his dad's touch. Has he got the little shuffles and the deft touch?

'He's got his shimmies, his little touches and that but I try to steer clear of comparisons,' says Hyde. 'As long as he enjoys it and learns something about the game and about himself, I'll be happy. It's not about whether he makes it or doesn't make it. That can kill the game for you if it's all you're thinking about.'

You're speaking like a dad there, Micah, not like a coach.

'Yeah, yeah, I know. But that's my philosophy with all of them, not just my son. They have to enjoy it because if there's one thing about football, it's that you're going to make mistakes. You. Are. Going. To. Make. Mistakes,' he repeats, more slowly for emphasis. 'It's how you respond that counts. If you enjoy the game you can learn from mistakes. If you don't, those mistakes will break you.'

\* \* \*

Micah Hyde grew up in Newham, not that far from Dagenham's ground, and from the age of eight to 14 he played for Ridgeway Rovers – a team that had the pick of the best youngsters from Essex and East London. One of his team-mates was David Beckham, who went on to play for Manchester United, Real Madrid and England, of course, although Hyde does not recall thinking that Beckham was set for stardom as a child.

'David wasn't a stand-out player at the time, and that's the truth,' says Hyde. 'He was just another good player in a good team. And we were a very good team – the best team not just in our area but for miles around. There would be scouts at pretty much every game. I remember Norwich City wanted to sign the whole team. They took us to Carrow Road and showed us around but for lads from east London, Norwich felt like a long, long way.

'There were several of us from Ridgeway Rovers who turned pro. Ryan Kirby went to Arsenal, Jason Brissett turned pro, Chris Day, who played in goal for Watford and is still at Stevenage, played for Ridgeway but he was a forward at the time. He didn't go in goal until later on. We had players who scored 40, 50 goals a season so Beckham didn't really stand out but he was always good with his dead-ball delivery. He took all our corners and free-kicks from when he was eight, so you could see he had quality but the reason he made it was not just his skill but his desire. His quality and a little bit of luck helped but he really, really wanted it. That's something I tell my players now – effort will get you to where you want to go. If it comes down to a choice between two players who have the same ability, the one who works hardest, the one who is most consistent, will go further. There are plenty of talented players who can't do it every game.'

Hyde joined Leyton Orient's youth team and spent several years there before the chance to join West Ham came along. Looking back, he realises he should have stayed at Orient.

'Definitely… Definitely. All day long,' he says. 'My mates were going to Spurs, Arsenal and blah blah blah and I was thinking, "What am I still doing at Orient?" When you're 14 or 15 you don't know anything but you think being at West Ham is going to be better than Orient.'

It didn't turn out like that. Hyde broke his ankle, got over-taken by other players while he recovered, and slipped out of the professional game, like so many others, at the age of 16. For most who make that downward journey in football's game of snakes and ladders, there is no way back, but Hyde was lucky. He spent a year playing Sunday league football for a team called Forest United, and played for his district and the county, and got picked up by Gary Johnson, who was then the manager of Cambridge United.

By 1997, Hyde was captain of Cambridge United's first team – the youngest skipper in England's four divisions at the time.

Gary Johnson had been appointed head of Watford's youth academy and, when Hyde caught Graham Taylor's eye, Johnson had no hesitation in vouching for the midfielder's character.

After a year spent stalking the corridors of power in a general manager role that did not seem to satisfy him, Graham Taylor had taken the reins of the team again. Kenny Jackett's bid to bounce straight back to the First Division had been hamstrung by chronic under-investment from the owner, Jack Petchey. Now a new consortium, with Elton John as its figurehead, had bought out Petchey and for the first time in years there was some money to spend.

And who better to spend it than Graham Taylor? Here was a man who had a knack of squeezing the last out of fading stars, picking up waifs and strays and players with a point to prove as well as those as yet unproven. Taylor's recruitment in the summer of 1997 ticked every box. While other teams in the Second Division may have shelled out bigger sums, Taylor was building a team. Ronny Rosenthal, who had played for Liverpool and Tottenham, was the most eye-catching arrival, although the clock was ticking on his career. Jason Lee, who had been ridiculed for his hairstyle by Baddiel and Skinner on their *Fantasy Football* show, needed a fresh start and dropped down from Nottingham Forest. Peter Kennedy had more or less been shown the door by Sam Allardyce at Notts County and was on the verge of returning to Northern Ireland in search of a proper job. And then there was Micah Hyde – a relative unknown whose name would not have been near the top of many fans' wish lists.

The initial fee of £150,000, which would rise to £250,000 after a certain number of appearances and other add-ons, did not break the bank, but it nevertheless represented a modest gamble for Watford.

Having said that, Hyde had attracted interest from other,

bigger clubs. Sheffield Wednesday's manager David Pleat wanted to speak to him but Hyde never made it as far as Yorkshire. It's a familiar tale. When Taylor wanted someone, he made sure he got in first and he made a compelling case. Hyde met Taylor and decided he didn't want to speak to anyone else, although Hyde can't quite put his finger on what it was that won him over.

'I spoke to Graham and that was it. I didn't go anywhere else. I honestly don't know what it was. I can't think of anything he said to me that stood out. It was just the way he made me feel. It must have been his charisma and personality. He explained what it was he wanted to achieve and he showed me around and that was it. It wasn't about money or anything like that. I'd made my mind up before we even discussed a contract.'

Taylor's knack for breaking a football team down into little partnerships and triangles and then assembling those component parts into a formidable unit is well known, but the midfield axis of Micah Hyde and Richard Johnson must be one of the most potent duos he ever put together for Watford.

Richard Johnson was 23 years old and still searching for his place in the team. Even then, in the summer of 1997, his career could have gone either way. The Australian had made his debut in December 1991, when still only 17, and established himself in the team under Glenn Roeder three years later. Johnson was a tenacious, often uncompromising presence in midfield. No one could dispute his work rate but sometimes the direction of his effort, like some of his passes, was misplaced. Every now and then he would score a spectacular long-range goal – the late winner against Taylor's Wolves team in 1994 springs to mind – that would more than compensate for any shortcomings. When Watford got relegated and Andy Hessenthaler vacated the engine room, the team desperately needed Johnson to step up but he was often struggling to do the work of two men.

Taylor identified Johnson's strengths but, just as importantly, he recognised the player's weaknesses and realised it was futile trying to make Johnson do a job for which he was not suited.

This is where Hyde came in. Johnson patrolled the midfield in hobnail boots whereas Hyde glided about it in carpet slippers. Johnson's game was based on closing down opponents and forcing mistakes but Taylor encouraged him to give up on the wild-goose chases and lost causes and be more disciplined. Hyde tackled using anticipation, not intimidation. Together they were a perfect fit and they lifted each other.

'We just clicked,' says Hyde. 'I think Richard appreciated the style I was bringing to him. He seemed a bit erratic in pre-season but he settled down and we just dovetailed well. I'm certainly not taking credit for that because he did things that I couldn't do and we fed off each other. Very quickly it felt like a partnership but it's pretty hard to explain why. We were two completely different personalities from two completely differ-ent backgrounds but we just got on well. On the pitch, I knew what he was going to do without having to speak to him. We didn't have long conversations about football, we just did it. If he was struggling, he didn't need to say anything, I just knew what to do to help him out and vice-versa.

'Sometimes we played a three, with Peter Kennedy in there with us. Johnno used to sit, Peter got wide, got his crosses in and I could get forward knowing that I could rely on Johnno. I knew he had my back. I'd nick the ball off people and try to get us going forward.'

For older fans, the way Hyde and Johnson worked together revived memories of Kenny Jackett and Les Taylor, who manned Graham Taylor's midfield when Watford took the top flight by storm in 1982-83. While many in the national press spent their time banging on about Watford's long-ball style, they missed the craft and industry of Jackett and Taylor and the way they dominated many of the best and most fêted midfielders in the country. Although they were operating at a lower level, there were similarities to the way Hyde and Johnson played. And there were plenty of people willing to dust off the old tag and label Taylor's Watford as long-ball merchants.

'People talk about Graham's teams being direct,' says Hyde, 'but we weren't direct. We were attacking. We wanted to score more goals than the other team and we wanted to get the ball down their end of the pitch quickly and create chances, but we didn't just hammer it from back to front. I wanted to play, I wanted the ball and I definitely didn't want it going over me or past me. We had players who knew their jobs. Graham wanted us to enjoy it. He was brilliant at man-management – brilliant, brilliant, brilliant. The belief he gave me was unreal. I came from the Third Division and I was in a team pushing to get promoted from the Second Division and within a couple of years I was in the Premier League. I believed in myself before, but he instilled something in us, a mind-set that we could do it.'

The 1997-98 season culminated in a showdown on the banks of the Thames. Fulham, managed by Kevin Keegan and coached by Ray Wilkins, were in the hunt for a play-off place, while Watford were already promoted but needed to win and hope that Bristol City failed to beat Preston North End in order to clinch the championship trophy.

'Fulham were a good side, who had a very strong midfield. They had Paul Bracewell [who had won the league title with Everton in 1985] and it was not a nothing game for them. They needed to win too, so to go there and play them off the park, which we did, was fantastic,' says Hyde. To put that achievement into context, it was only the third Football League title Watford had won, after the Fourth Division in 1960 and the Third Division in 1969. The band of players who have won a trophy for Watford is a pretty exclusive club.

Stepping up to the First Division held few fears for Hyde or Johnson. Graham Taylor saw to that. 'We went into every game with a positive mentality. It wasn't Graham's style to go away somewhere and try to nick a point. Even if we were up against a good team, we tried to play our game. Johnno didn't want to be second best in midfield and I didn't want to be second best either. I certainly didn't want to get embarrassed. Before kick-off, we'd look across at the opposition and I'd be thinking: "I want to be better than you," and Johnno would be thinking the same. If you have that combination in the middle of the park it can be very hard to beat.'

It was not a conventional promotion push. After a strong start and a consistent autumn, Watford found themselves second in the table as winter approached. But after Christmas the pace slowed and they managed only two wins in 13 games. Then came the surge back into the play-off places, the dramatic penalty shoot-out victory over Birmingham and the club's first win at Wembley. Confidence throughout the squad was sky-high and Taylor was determined, as far as possible, to give the men who had earned promotion the chance to prove they could survive in the Premiership.

Taylor knew that not everyone would make it but he said that some of the players, having made it to the top flight, would never have to play at a lower level again. Looking at the squad, the players that comment applied to were Hyde, Johnson and perhaps Paul Robinson. Hyde may have jumped from the bottom division to the Premiership in consecutive seasons, but he felt ready to go up against the best midfielders in the country: David Beckham and Paul Scholes at Manchester United, Patrick Vieira and Emmanuel Petit at Arsenal, Didier Deschamps at Chelsea and Steven Gerrard at Liverpool. He's not sure the rest of the team was relishing the challenge as much.

Hyde was injured for the first two games, which Watford lost to Wimbledon and Sunderland, but he was fit to face Liverpool at Anfield. That afternoon ranks as one of the greatest away wins in the club's history. Watford had never won a league game at either Liverpool or Everton, but Tommy Mooney's early goal and a brilliant display by Chris Day, Ridgeway Rovers' old centre forward, in goal secured a 1-0 victory.

'I wasn't daunted by playing in the Premiership at all, not one bit, but I had players in my team that were,' says Hyde. 'I knew I would have more time on the ball. As a midfielder you get more time on the ball but it's harder to make that time count. When I watch Premier League football now, and the midfielder isn't doing anything, I think: "How can you not get into the game? How can you not want the ball and go and get it?" I enjoyed it.

'I don't think all my team-mates enjoyed it. After games I was frustrated because the team could have done better, I'm sure. But we had players that were in awe. They respected the opposition too much, for me. My personal performances were, I thought, okay, but I was disappointed in some of my team-mates. Not all of them, but some of them got there and thought, "Well, we're Watford – we're not good enough for this." There were games we lost that we wouldn't have lost the year before, goals we conceded that we wouldn't have conceded in the lower division.'

The Premiership tends to get on top of promoted teams if they allow it to. After wins against Liverpool and Bradford City came three consecutive 1-0 defeats, to Aston Villa and at Leicester and West Ham. Close but no cigar. Then came another afternoon that offered hope that Watford might just keep their noses above water, when Allan Smart's goal stunned Chelsea at Vicarage Road. But after battling hard at Arsenal before losing 1-0 and after leading Leeds at half-time before slipping to a 2-1 defeat, the tide rushed in and swept the Hornets off their feet. Narrow defeats became comprehensive ones. A 4-1 thumping at Manchester United, a 3-1 defeat at home to Middlesbrough and a 4-0 thrashing at Coventry City left the team gasping for air.

'A lot of the players were too happy to say, "Oh well, we got beat by Newcastle cause Shearer scored a worldie," or whatever, but for me that's not good enough,' says Hyde. As it happens, Shearer's 'worldie' came in a 1-1 draw against Newcastle at Vicarage Road, but Hyde's point stands. 'I don't accept that as an excuse,' says Hyde. 'I don't care how he scores his goal. I wasn't interested in that. My sons, my two boys, ask, "Have you got so-and-so's shirt?" and I say, "I wasn't there to swap shirts." It never crossed my mind. I didn't want to look dotingly into their faces; that wasn't what I was about. Maybe I should have but it just wasn't my mentality to go and ask [Thierry] Henry for his shirt. I respected him, don't get me wrong, he's a great player but I wanted to play as well. I wasn't in awe of people that much that I'd want their shirts.'

Taylor tried to work the old magic again. He brought in Charlie Miller – a mercurial, Gazza-esque midfielder from Rangers, whose reputation arrived at Vicarage Road before he did – and a Frenchman, Xavier Gravelaine, who was undoubtedly gifted but tended to vanish into thin air during away games.

'Charlie was a lovely fella, a great guy,' says Hyde. 'A lovely footballer, with great skills, but he and Graham didn't see eye-to-eye at the time. Charlie wasn't for Graham because there wasn't enough end product. He was a little too flighty for Graham.' And Gravelaine? 'Just not fit enough. He had great touches and he could put it in the top corner but he didn't do enough in games. You need to work a little bit off the ball in the English game. I don't mean like a workhorse but you have to be in a position to affect the game.'

Watford didn't exactly exit the Premiership kicking and screaming. Victory against Coventry City on the final day of the season was their first for nine games – a run that included consecutive 3-2 defeats to Arsenal and Manchester United. The United game was particularly frustrating because Watford were 1-0 up at half-time. Heidar Helguson had given the Hornets the lead and Hyde was running the show from midfield – so much so that Alex Ferguson brought Dwight Yorke on at half-time and dropped him into a deep position to disrupt Hyde's influence. It was partially successful but United still needed to do more. As the second half wore on they began to focus their attention on Hyde. Nicky Butt took the task of trying to get under Hyde's skin and eventually he snapped.

'He kept niggling away,' says Hyde. 'He kicked me a few times and he was saying stuff to me. It was derogatory but it wasn't nasty. Footballers give each other stick all the time.'

Like sledging in cricket?

'Yeah. It was pretty innocent but he was going on and on. "We're Man United, we're going to win the league and you're going down. Enjoy it at Crewe," or whatever. Usually I'd let it go over my head and get on with my game but it wound me up and we clashed. He pushed me, I think, and I retaliated. I walked into it and I take responsibility for my own actions. I should have just winked at him and carried on playing my football. If people respect you enough to try to disturb your game, you've got to be above that. Graham didn't say anything to me afterwards, because he knew that I knew I'd let myself down, massively. Not just myself but the team.'

Hyde and Butt were both sent off in the 65th minute. Three minutes later Yorke, now enjoying the freedom of the midfield, equalised for United. Seven minutes after that Ryan Giggs put United ahead and although Tommy Smith dragged the Hornets level, the ten men always looked vulnerable. The inevitable United winner, scored by Jordi Cruyff, came four minutes from the end.

The Premiership had taught Watford some painful lessons but Hyde had acquitted himself well. He looked at home in the top flight, which made it all the more surprising when Graham Taylor spent £2.25m – a club record fee – on Tottenham's Danish midfielder Allan Nielsen that summer. It looked like a bit of a slap in the face.

'I welcomed it,' says Hyde. 'I play better if there's a bit of competition. I liked him as a player but sometimes he could be a bit frustrating for me. I used to think of myself as a bit of a purist on the ball and he used to frustrate me and give the ball away a bit much, or he'd get in a position where I couldn't find him. But he was an international, by the way, so let's not get carried away. The goals he brought to the team and the way he arrived late in the box, sort of Lampard-ish, was very, very good, so he didn't really change what Johnno and I did.'

* * *

It was early August 2000 and the team had just played a friendly against Walsall at Tamworth's ground. The players were sitting on the coach waiting for Graham Taylor, when his assistant, Kenny Jackett, got on board at the front.

'Micah, Charlie, the gaffer wants to see you in the changing room,' said Jackett.

Hyde and Charlie Miller looked at each other, wondering why the manager could want them but not the rest of the squad.

They got up to walk towards the front doors of the coach.

'No, no, just get off at the back,' said Jackett.

'As we got off at the back, we saw the gaffer get on at the front,' says Hyde, smiling at the memory. 'The doors closed and the coach just drove off, leaving us standing in the car park. We thought they must be winding us up and that the coach would be back in a minute. We didn't know what we'd done wrong, we just thought they were having a joke with us so we were laughing away.'

But the coach didn't come back. Hyde and Miller had been abandoned at Tamworth Football Club, a hundred miles or more from home. Their phones and wallets were on the coach. They were stranded.

Then it dawned on Hyde why the manager had left them.

A few days earlier, the squad had posed for the traditional pre-season team photograph. Hyde and Miller were sitting next to each other in the front row. 'We put our hands on each other's knees so it looked like he had a black hand and I had a white hand,' says Hyde. The problem was no one spotted it until they'd been printed to sell in the club shop. 'Graham found out and went ballistic. We heard later he'd gone absolutely ballistic but he hadn't said anything to us. We'd played Walsall and everything was fine but Graham decided to have the last laugh.'

Hyde and Miller called for a taxi from the office at Tamworth's ground and made the long, expensive trip back to Hertfordshire where Miller's wife paid the driver. 'I meant to pay him back the next day, but I forgot,' says Hyde. 'But I'd bought him so many rounds anyway…'

Spirits were high and Watford were among the bookmakers' favourites to make an immediate return to the Premiership. Although Hyde was in and out of the team, when he did play he made a big impact, scoring in the 4-1 win against Sheffield United, getting two in a thrilling 4-3 victory over Blackburn Rovers at Ewood Park and netting both goals in a sublime 2-0 win over Nottingham Forest.

It looked as if Watford and Fulham were going to

run away with the two automatic promotion places. On November 5, Watford were top, a point clear of Fulham, and eight ahead of third-placed Birmingham City, with a game in hand. And then the wheels fell off. It was one of the most spectacular collapses in the club's history. In their first 15 games, they had won 12 and drawn three. After that they took one point from the next eight matches, slipping from the top of the table to eighth. The lowest point was a 5-0 thrashing at Fulham on Boxing Day – a mauling Hyde was not spared.

Hyde cannot explain why things went so spectacularly wrong. 'I can't give you a definitive answer. As a group we'd been together a while. I don't know what it was. It wasn't like we weren't trying to win games but there are so many things you can't put your finger on in football.'

The team could not arrest the decline and, in March, Graham Taylor announced he would retire at the end of the season. Hyde was named on the bench for Taylor's last match as Watford manager, at Burnley, and came on near the end. It had been public knowledge for a few weeks that Taylor's replacement would be the Italian, Gianluca Vialli. Although excited by Vialli's impending arrival, Hyde was sad that Taylor was leaving.

'He showed faith in me and I like to think I repaid that faith. We had a really good relationship. He loved me. He'd say things in team meetings – not just to me, he loved Peter [Kennedy] as well. He loved Peter when Peter was firing, scoring all those goals. After that, he didn't love Peter so much and he started leaving him out. I was waiting for him to turn around and do to me what he did to Peter but he seemed to like me for the duration.' Hyde laughs an affectionate laugh. I suggest he was the team's teacher's pet, something he dismisses. 'No, no – I was just an ordinary player – but he did mention me a lot in the team meetings. He called me the barometer of the team because I was the level that he wanted all the team to be playing at. He'd say things like that and it made me feel good. He used to say he wished he had 11 Micahs. But don't get me wrong – when I wasn't playing well, he let me know that too but he knew how to man-manage people. He instilled confidence in me.

'Kenny Jackett was very strict with everyone, but what a brilliant coach. He's the best coach I've ever had. His sessions had a serious intensity. I've said from the beginning, whatever team Kenny Jackett has, he will be successful. He's been good at Swansea, Millwall and Wolves but he ain't one to put his arm around you and say, "How are you doing, bro?" Then there was Luther Blissett who made everything fun. He was so good at coaching attacking sessions – not just for the forwards, but for the whole team. But Graham was the boss. He could be aloof but he was such a good manager. As a person playing under him, how could I not learn? I've tried to take something from all three of them into my own coaching.'

So what of Vialli, who had won Serie A and the Champions League as a player with Juventus before coming to England and winning the FA Cup, the European Cup Winners' Cup and the League Cup with Chelsea? As Chelsea manager, he'd won the FA Cup again before falling foul of Ken Bates, the club's axe-happy chairman. His appointment was quite a coup for Watford. Vialli added glamour and promised excitement.

Before the players returned for pre-season training, Vialli had drawn up a list of those he wanted to keep and those he wanted out. Club captain Robert Page was one who was ousted in a manner that did not befit his service to the cause. Hyde, who had a contract, seemed to fall between the two lists.

Vialli inherited Nielsen, Paolo Vernazza, Hyde and John-son – although the Australian was on the sidelines with a long-term injury – but set about adding more midfielders. In came Stephen Hughes from Everton, Stephen Glass from Newcastle, although he operated mostly in wide positions, and the highly-rated David Noble, on loan from Arsenal. Suddenly Hyde found himself slipping down the pecking order.

'He didn't like me – I don't mean personally, I mean as a player. I was one that he didn't fancy,' says Hyde.

Did Vialli make it obvious? 'Yeah. Look, I wasn't a child, I was a professional, so it wasn't a problem that he didn't like me. I knew what I had to do to be liked and get in the team and that was do my job well, but he made it obvious who he fancied and who he didn't. But I changed that. I changed his mentality. I went and did what I had to do and I got in his team.'

Hyde played in Vialli's first match as boss – an expectation-busting 3-0 defeat to Kevin Keegan's Manchester City – and kept his place in the team. Vialli's methods were new for Watford's players. The squad would train, then head to Sopwell House hotel in St Albans for lunch and a nap, then train again. There were coaches and fitness coaches and performance analysts but the results were not good.

'He implemented all these changes to make us better and because it was the only thing he knew. There was no right or wrong to what Vialli was doing but it's the results you get on the park that count.

'People can complicate football. I think it's a very simple game. You've either got the ball or they have – it's as simple as that. All this talk about how to keep the ball and how to go about getting it back is too much. Vialli came in and wanted to implement things straight away but, for me, he didn't understand the league we were in or have a feel for it. He brought in players that didn't fit.

'There was no penetration. There wasn't enough encouragement to go and play football. There was too much overthinking. He brought in players of a certain quality but he also brought in players who added none. None.'

Don't hold back there, Micah. Name names.

'No, I wouldn't name names because we're all professionals.'

I can probably guess. Ramon Vega, Patrick Blondeau, Stephen Hughes. Hyde won't be drawn. There's not even a flicker on his poker face.

'They were good players wherever they'd been before but perhaps that was because they were used to a slower tempo. What we were doing was too ponderous, too over-thought at times. We should just have played the game. Vialli went on about the opposition a lot and under Graham we really didn't worry about the opposition. We didn't really care about them or what they were going to do. Okay, so if they had a particular way of playing or something that we needed to know about, he'd tell us, but we didn't focus on the opposition – we focused on us. We might do a little bit of work on our shape on Thursday or Friday but our training was about what we were going to do to beat whatever team was in front of us. With Vialli, he flipped it and we spent a lot of time working on how to stop the other team. It was a very European way of thinking and it was all good stuff. His football knowledge was brilliant – brilliant – but for the league we were in it didn't work.'

* * *

That summer Vialli left, the broadcaster ITV Digital collapsed leaving many First Division clubs struggling to plug a black hole in their finances. Within weeks of the new season starting, with Ray Lewington promoted from a coaching role to manager, the squad was being asked to take a wage cut.

'The general feeling was uncertainty,' says Hyde. 'Watford had been a nice, stable, family club and players don't necessarily know everything that's going on so we were thinking, "What's going on here?" You don't know what wages everyone is getting but I think we were generally on good contracts and we were wondering why they had over-budgeted. Generally, though, I think the feeling in the dressing room was that we'd take the deferral and hope we'd get the money back. I've been in changing rooms where they want to take £10 more for your lunch and the players are like, "No, no, no, that's not happening," but we were all right with it. There were a few jokes about giving Elton a ring to bail us out and he did a concert at the ground, didn't he? I had a young family but I wasn't too worried about it. Maybe if I'd been older, getting towards the end of my career, it would have been on my mind more.'

Lewington had an unenviable task. His budget was cut over and over but he had to keep the team in the First Division. Inevitably, it led to a more cautious style of play and Hyde felt he began to drift.

'For a while I felt like I needed something new because he wasn't testing me enough as a player,' says Hyde. 'Ray's a great coach – a good, good, good coach. What he's doing now for England fits him like a glove but, in my opinion, as a number one? I'm not sure. I love Ray. He was as honest as the day is long and I never had any problem with him but I wanted a manager to push me. I wanted to be told to, you know, liven up. Realistically, in his head, I think he knew the limits of what we could achieve as a team but I think you've got to maybe project a different message to the players, because then maybe we might finish above that. The message coming across, to me at least, was safety first, precaution, and no team is going to be successful like that.'

Watford reached the FA Cup semi-final in Lewington's first season, losing to Southampton at Villa Park, but Hyde barely remembers the game or the day. 'Probably because we lost it,' he says. 'I remember the positives, and I remember Wembley and all that, but not too many of the negatives.'

Hyde left Watford in the summer of 2004, after seven years at the club, and he went with mixed feelings. On one hand he didn't want to leave, but he needed to rejuvenate his career and he didn't feel Lewington wanted him to stick around – perhaps partly because his would have been a good salary to get off the books. 'They offered me a contract but they kind of opened the door a bit to see if I would walk through it,' he says. 'So I had to go. That's football, but I'd have liked to have gone out with a bit more of a flourish. Maybe I overstayed my welcome there a little bit.'

A couple of years earlier, Hyde thought he might follow Graham Taylor to Aston Villa. Taylor had come out of retirement to take charge of Villa again and Hyde half-expected a call. 'I felt that was my time to go. I thought I could have done a job in the Premiership at that time.'

When he finally left, he went to Burnley, who had only nine players on the books when he arrived. A year or so later, he was joined at Turf Moor by Gifton Noel-Williams. Hyde enjoyed three years at Burnley before moving to Peterborough United, then on to Barnet, where he played with Paul Furlong. When he retired from professional football in 2010, he found it tough to give up the game and turned out for several non-league teams, including St Albans City, where he played with Furlong again.

'I've never been one for the gym, or for running or for walking around a golf course. I just don't get enjoyment from it. My missus said she wasn't having me sitting around the house and whatnot, so I started playing again, just for the enjoyment, to play and keep fit. But obviously there comes a time when you can't do it no more and you have to call it a day.'

Hyde's passion for the game makes the transformation to coaching an obvious one but I wonder how far he thinks he can go. The elephant in the room is that the percentage of black footballers playing in England's top four divisions far outweighs the percentage of black coaches and managers.

'I'm glad you've brought that up because I would have brought it up if you hadn't,' he says. 'I am not one to run away from that particular topic. I may not get a job so I might as well just speak my mind and say how it is. It's clear chairmen don't trust black managers and that has to change. That. Has. To. Change. And it will change; I just hope it changes in my time. I'm not going to be one to sit around and wait for it to happen for me. I need to do this to the best of my ability, get the qualifications, and when I am ready I will apply for jobs. Maybe after this year I will, and I'll be pitting myself against some of my peers. I'll be up against people who have no more qualifications than me so there's no reason why I can't be competing with them. I want to actively find out if there is this prejudice out there and if there are going to be doors slammed in my face all the time.

'At the moment what I see is not good. I've got people in front of me, people who have played at a high level, who have managed – black managers like Chris Hughton and Chris Powell – who were given opportunities and who got sacked. Maybe they won't get the opportunity to manage again and that is what has to change. I see managers out there who fail repeatedly – white managers who fail repeatedly – but they get another job and then, when they are successful, people forget the failures and how many times they've lost a job before. Everyone fails sometimes but are we allowed, as black people, to fail?

'They're not giving us enough time or opportunities to fail. Now, I'm not saying I am going to be a great manager, or that I'm going to win a championship. Maybe I'm not but in order to succeed we have to be given chances. John Barnes is one case, Luther Blissett's been looking for a job for years – he can't get one – Michael Johnson has applied for every single job and can't get one. Black managers are not being given the same

opportunities to fail as white managers and that is all we want –
the same opportunity. We'll never get anywhere if you get one
chance and that's it. If ten of us get a job, three or four will do
well, and that's the same as white managers.

'It can be daunting to see what's in front of you once you
cross over into coaching and management. I might pass away,
die, and nothing's changed. My sons would have to go through
the same rigmarole and I'd hate that to be the case. That's my
ultimate fear – that my career will be over, I'll be an old man
and my sons will be going through the same stuff, so it's up
to my generation and the one below me to try to implement
change, to ask for a chance in a respectful, professional way. I'd
be happy if you said that in 20 years' time there might be 50
black coaches in the league. It might be too late for me but I'd
know my sons, and their sons, would have a chance. We need to
see change. We need to see black people in the boardroom.

'I think back to Graham Taylor and he didn't care about
colour. There was never a split in the dressing room. We didn't
have Gift, Wayne Andrews, Jason Lee and me at one table and
Tommy Mooney, Pagey and Johnno at another, and that's not
common at every club. At some clubs you still get the black
players sticking together. The attitude comes from the top. It
doesn't even need to be said; it's just an attitude that we're all
the same and we all get the same chances.'

I ask if he'd like to return to Watford one day, as manager.

'Yeah, I love Watford. Everyone who knows me knows that.
I'd love to go back there one day. I've no qualms saying that
because if it doesn't happen it doesn't change my life. I have no
qualms saying what I'd like to happen in my life. I wouldn't say
it's a dream because a dream is something that's not attainable
and that is attainable. I am trying, trying, trying to do that.'

So what sort of coach is Micah Hyde?

'I coach the kids and I try to tell them that hard work is the most important thing. It's hard because they're already thinking about the lifestyle football can bring and you have to prepare them because in a group of 20, one might make it. That's the hard fact. So we have a black boots policy here – no yellow boots, or orange boots – and we don't have anyone with their socks over their knees. Them things are banned.'

But Micah, you were fond of coloured boots.

'Yeah, but I was a professional player, I liked that pressure.'

Funnily enough, Hyde led Graham Taylor to ban bladed boots when they first became popular. He slipped and missed a chance in a game against Sheffield United and Taylor blamed Hyde's boots, which had bladed soles rather than studs. Hyde laughs. 'Yeah, no one was allowed to wear them after that. That was typical Graham, that. He was the gaffer.'

A few weeks before our interview, the old double-act had pulled on their boots again and turned out for a Watford legends team in a charity match at Wealdstone. It was the first time Hyde and Johnson had played together since Watford's League Cup tie against Bournemouth in August 2003. So did they turn on the old magic?

'Whoa, I don't know about the old magic,' he says, flashing a grin. 'I tell you, the exterior might look good but the interior ain't as good as it used to be. We done all right. I like to play but my knees have gone now. They can't let me do what I'd like to do, which is a bit frustrating. I was never one to run around at a hundred miles an hour so the pace we play now suits me. I get the ball to do the work.

'My missus came to watch and she said: "Luther's putting you to shame. He's 50-odd and he's running around and you're not even moving." Yeah, Luther is as fit as a fiddle – just the same as he was, always so enthusiastic.'

And what about Johnno?

'Oh, you know Johnno. He still likes a tackle.'

# CRAIG RAMAGE

**On his relationship with the fans**
'I was always waiting for them
to start singing the old *One Craig
Ramage*. I didn't like it if someone
else got a louder chant!'

# 3

Craig Ramage was the archetypal midfield stroller. He could glide past opponents and spot passes no one else could see.

At his very best, he was the team's inspirational puppetmaster, pulling the strings and making things happen.

He divided opinion, as a lot of talented players do, because his work-rate did not always match his ingenuity.

But the simple fact was that not everyone could be as Cool as Craig.

# CRAIG RAMAGE

New Year's Eve 1994. Night is falling on Vicarage Road. Elsewhere parties are getting started and the Champagne is on ice but no one is in the mood to celebrate here. Watford are labouring to a 2-2 draw against Port Vale, a team struggling at the bottom of the table, but playing, for one day only, like title contenders. Typical. Absolutely typical.

Injury time is ticking away like the countdown to midnight. Auld Lang Syne will be tinged with disappointment later.

And then something magical happens. Craig Ramage bursts forward from midfield with an energy that suggests he's spotted something no one else can see. He meets the ball and lobs it over the Port Vale keeper into the net. 3-2.

Ramage continues his run past the goalposts and into the arms of the mob of delighted Watford fans. If he wants to celebrate New Year in Watford town centre, he won't have to pay for a drink all night.

Let's get this party started.

* * *

There was not a lot to cheer if you were a Watford fan in the mid-Nineties. This was an era when the pitches were still heavy in winter. The Sky-led gentrification of football had not yet trickled down to the likes of us. The middle of all but the best pitches turned into a heavy porridge of mud and sand between about mid-October and late March.

For years – since Graham Taylor's departure in 1987, in fact – it had felt like Watford were stuck in a rut. The going always seemed to be heavy underfoot. There was the odd moment to lift the spirits – a rare cup win, or a brief flirtation with the top half of the table – but mostly these were seasons of drudgery. An aimless plod to nowhere.

And while there were players who could raise a smile every now and then, we knew that if they got too good they wouldn't be around long. Mostly, we loved Watford's players because of their flaws, not despite them.

And then Craig Ramage arrived. It was as if someone had turned on a spotlight that picked him out in the centre circle and then followed him, bathing him in a warm light, as he sashayed around the pitch.

The fact that Ramage arrived during a barren period that seemed like it might never end is significant. We were crying out for a bit of excitement and invention and here was an artisan, a creative spirit, who could get pulses racing. When he felt like it.

As supporters we'd always been a bit mistrustful of the obviously gifted. Even during the great rise to the top flight and beyond, the club's most successful years, we voted for goal-keepers, defenders and midfielders in the annual player of the season poll. We went for industry over artistry. Steve Sims, Les Taylor, Wilf Rostron, John McClelland and Tony Coton were all fine players – Hornets hall of fame material – but the flakier brilliance of John Barnes, Nigel Callaghan or Luther Blissett did not get quite the same recognition.

With his floppy blond hair parted in the middle Ramage could almost have been the front man in a Britpop band. The singer and lead guitarist, naturally. He wore his shirt untucked at the waist (something that would have driven Graham Taylor mad) and he sauntered about in the same casual manner. But he could throw an opponent off the scent with the drop of a shoulder and he could split a defence in two with a pass that looked complex and yet simple at the same time.

It's ironic that Ramage acknowledges his best form came when the season was a couple of months old, as the days got colder and the pitches heavier. With his eye for a pass you might think he'd have been happier on a surface as smooth as a billiard table but he seemed to come alive on the roughest of pitches, flicking the ball over the divots and using the unpredictability of churned-up turf to his advantage.

Craig Ramage was a cult hero. The love for him was not universal. Not everyone worshipped him because not everyone *got* him. For some, his refusal to chase back, his inability to commit the same energy to defence as attack, and the way he seemed to switch from lackadaisical to inspired and back again, was simply too frustrating.

Ramage was the sort of player who could have you tearing your hair in exasperation and within a second have you on your feet celebrating a goal. Why couldn't he be that good all the time?

The brilliant fanzine, *Clap Your Hands, Stamp Your Feet*, captured his character when they commissioned the *Watford Observer*'s cartoonist Terry Challis to come up with an illustration for their 'Cool as Craig' T-shirts. (Ramage's wife still has one, he tells me later).

So how did such an outrageous talent end up joining struggling Watford for just £90,000 in February 1994? To put it bluntly, he was damaged goods.

\* \* \*

I was living in Hastings, training to become a journalist, when Ramage signed for Watford. I did a bit of background reading and was encouraged and concerned in equal measure by what I learned. He was an English under-21 international – a 23-year-old midfielder with flair who had been mentioned in the same breath as Paul Gascoigne. But on the other hand, he'd played fewer than 50 first-team games in almost six years because of two lengthy knee injuries.

I remembered the words of the legendary Terry Challis, who would puncture my enthusiasm whenever the Hornets signed a new player during those gloomy, seemingly hopeless years with the phrase: 'If he was Pele, he wouldn't be coming here, would he?'

Weekends could be bleak on the south coast in winter. Living away from your football team, even just for a few months, strengthens the bond somehow and so it was not a difficult decision to drive up to The Valley to see Ramage's debut against Charlton Athletic. The Addicks were in the hunt for promotion, Watford were struggling at the other end of the table.

Watford lost 2-1. It was the sort of result that could be explained, if not justified, by the opposition's lofty league position but, in truth, Charlton were just as awful as we were. They lost nine of the next ten.

Ramage was not Pele but on his debut he showed he had flashes of something we were not used to seeing.

'I had hunger and desire when I joined Watford,' he says when we meet at his house in Derbyshire. 'I felt like I was a big fish in a small pond but I knew I had to show what I was all about. I think people looked at me on my debut and said, "Jesus, maybe we've got a player here?" I got rave reviews and I think our players realised that they could give me the ball and trust me with it.'

I can't say I was convinced that first day. It struck me he was the last thing we needed. What we needed was another nine Andy Hessenthalers – people who would roll up their sleeves and run, scrap and defy relegation by sheer force of will. There was no room in the bottom six of the First Division for midfielders like Craig Ramage. He looked like too much of a luxury to me.

I was completely wrong, of course. Although it was counter-intuitive, Ramage was exactly what we were desperate for. We needed someone who could create chances, build excitement and make us feel good about ourselves because these were desperate times.

Three days before that Charlton game an advert had appeared in the *Daily Telegraph*. I didn't see it at the time and I doubt many, if any, Watford fans realised its significance. It read: 'For Sale. Southern English First Division Football Club. Interested parties with proven funds only should apply in writing.' We had no idea at the time that the anonymous advert had been placed by Jack Petchey although it didn't take a genius to work out that the owner's interest, barely apparent at the best of times, had waned completely.

A couple of weeks later, Watford lost 3-0 at home to Grimsby Town in front of 5,109 people. Angered by the team's meek surrender, some fans ran on the pitch and a few tried to 'storm' the directors' box, even though Petchey wasn't actually at the game.

So Ramage's arrival was not the panacea. It would take a little while for his genius to become obvious to all.

\* \* \*

Craig Ramage is a Derby lad, born and bred. He bought a house not far from the city when he was a young man still playing for Derby, stayed there even though his career took him as far south as Watford and as far north as Bradford, and paid if off by the time he was 31. Recently he's been working for BBC Radio Derby as a commentator. Derby is still in his blood, but so is Watford, because he played more games for the Hornets than anyone else.

He had trained with Derby County since he was a child and signed for them when he was 14. Scouts from other clubs in the East Midlands had been interested, but Ramage's dad made him go to Nottingham Forest, Notts County and Leicester to have a look around before signing for Derby. When the Rams made their offer, there was no decision to be made.

'I was a Derby lad, so I wanted to play for them,' he says. 'They made a big fuss of me and I signed on the pitch, with my parents, before a game at the Baseball Ground. It was against Plymouth Argyle, I think. They gave me a black Derby County bomber jacket, like one of those shiny American football jackets. It had a Rams logo on and I was dead proud of it. I went into school in it, like I was in America or something.

'The club said I'd sign as an apprentice pro at 16 but by then I was burned out. I played for my school, for the district and Derby Boys. I was training with Derby County and on Sundays I played for my club Chesapeake. I scored 83 goals for them one season. So when I got to 16, Derby offered me a six-month contract because I was burned out. My heart went a little bit and I started seeing there were other things than football. It could have gone either way. My dad said, "They're going to give you six months so you have time to sort yourself out," and after a couple of months of going to bed at seven o'clock every night I got back in shape and I was flying.'

Derby signed him for another two years and before long Ramage got into the reserve team. When Ramage turned 18, the Derby manager, Arthur Cox, was looking to get him some more experience.

'Coxy dragged me in the office and said he was sending me to Lincoln on loan. They were in the Fourth Division and he said, "Go and get some scars on your face." So I went there and trained a few days. I was taking the mickey out of these big centre-halves, nutmegging them and stuff. I'd come from Derby, who were in the First Division by now, and we had some top players, so it all seemed quite easy at Lincoln.

'I played in their reserves and I was getting kicked about a bit but I thought I was having a worldie, I did. I thought, 'Oh, I'll be in the first team after this." I got to the ground for the game, a good crowd was in, and Colin Murphy, the manager, said to me, "I don't want you here, son. You can get yourself home tonight." So instead of playing in the game I was driving home.

'When I got back to Derby, Murphy had written a letter to Coxy saying, "He's an arrogant bastard. He stands around with his hands in his pockets. He's not for me." He gave me some right stick.' Ramage laughs and for a moment you can see how easy it must've been for such a talented youngster to stray over the line that divides youthful self-belief from cockiness.

Next, Arthur Cox sent him to Wigan. 'I was there a week and the manager, Ray Mathias, got the bullet, so I experienced that side of the game. He came in, with a tear in his eye, and said, "See you, lads." I had a great three months at Wigan, even though we were struggling at the bottom of the Third Division. I made my league debut, played ten games and scored a couple of goals.'

Back at Derby again, his first professional contract was running out and when the club offered him another two-year deal, Ramage left it sitting on the table for a few weeks. Arthur Cox asked him: 'Are you signing this contract or not?'

Ramage replied: 'Well, I'd like a bit more cash.'

Derby withdrew the offer and put him on a week-to-week contract instead. It might have been disastrous for the 19-year-old, playing hardball with the manager and losing out but he soon broke into the first team and was playing against Manchester United and Liverpool.

'I had an agent,' he says. 'I was probably one of the first to get an agent. They were just coming into the game at the time. Arthur wanted me to sign this contract and he said: "If you haven't signed it by five o'clock, I'm lowering the offer."

'My agent gets on the phone and tells Arthur I'm worth more than they are offering. Arthur calls me and says: "Look, we don't need to get agents involved. I'm sending you something in the post tonight. Make sure you come and sign in the morning.

'I couldn't sleep all night, and then I opened the post and it's Arthur's offer. I was quite happy with that but when I went in I thought I'd try for another hundred quid. I wanted to buy my first house and stand on my own two feet. So Arthur and I are standing there haggling. "Fifty," he said. "Seventy-five," I said. "Fifty," he said. In the end I agreed to the extra £50 and he dragged me up to the secretary's office to sign.'

One of Ramage's team-mates at Derby was Nigel Callaghan, the former Watford winger. 'His crossing was frightening – unbelievable quality every time. You could tell him where you wanted it and he'd hit a spot with power, pace or he could float it in and cut out the defenders and the goalkeeper. Brilliant. He didn't look quick but he could glide past defenders. That showed me what you could do if you could make the ball do what you wanted it to do.

'I loved Cally because he was the only player with bigger calves than mine! People used to say to me, "Do you want some more air in them?"'

Following relegation, Derby's wealthy owner, Lionel Pickering, was financing a push back towards the top flight. The Rams had invested heavily and his injuries had moved Ramage towards the exit door.

But for his injuries, and the lengthy recovery process, he would have left earlier.

The problems started in 1991 when he was playing for Derby reserves against Nottingham Forest. Ramage ran across to close down the Forest full-back, Gary Charles, as he was about to clear the ball up the line. 'I blocked the clearance and I caught my studs in the turf, heard a crack and went down in a heap,' he says.

An exploratory operation showed he'd torn his ligaments. 'They said I'd be out for two or three months but that I might get away with it if I did some rehab work to build it up. A tear is not as bad as a snap and because I was quite slight, there was a chance I'd be able to come back quickly.'

By the time he was playing again, a transfer to Notts County was on the cards. 'Notts were still in the First Division and we were in the Second Division by now, so it would have been a move up for me,' Ramage says. 'They were going to swap me for Tommy Johnson and Notts wanted me to play up front for them. I was playing a reserve game for Derby at Notts County just before the transfer was due to go through. I had my agent sitting in the stand with Derek Pavis, the Notts chairman, and as I came off at half-time I gave them a little wink because I was giving their centre-half the run-around. In the last few minutes of the second half I went up for a header and when I landed, my knee buckled under me and then gave way and that was that. The next day I went in for an operation on my cruciate ligaments and I was out for six months.'

He came back just in time for the end of the season and forced his way into the team as Derby won six of their last eight games, just missing out on automatic promotion before losing to Kenny Dalglish's Blackburn Rovers in the semi-final of the play-offs. 'Coxy left me out of that one, which was disappointing because I thought I was playing well.'

Over the summer, Ramage was called up to play for an England under-21 side in the Toulon tournament in the south of France. 'I'd been away with England, I'd trained really well, I felt fit and the Derby gaffer sat us down and said, "Everyone here has got a chance to get in the first-team." Then he looked round the group, looked at me and said, "Except you, Ramage."

'He was just trying to keep my feet on the ground but it made me think, "Right, I'll show you," and by the time we got to the final pre-season game, against Stoke, I'd got in the team. You know if you get into the side for that last game of pre-season then you're in the 11 for the first game of the season so I was feeling great. In the first five minutes, Darren Wassell played the ball to me and it was a bit of a short one and I got absolutely clobbered by their defender. I was winded and couldn't breathe and I had the physio on so I could get my breath back. I was still getting over that when the ball came to me. I rode one tackle, then I tried to change direction and my studs got caught in the turf again. My leg went one way and my body went the other way.

'So I had six months out with this knee, seven months out with the other one,' he says, pointing to one leg then the other. 'I had the Macintosh operation where they took seven inches of tissue from my thigh and made it into a new ligament and wrapped it round to keep the knee solid,' he says. 'They've got better operations now so they don't tend to do it anymore because after a while you can stretch it and the knee becomes unstable again. But yes, I've got scars. It's like a shark bite all the way up there,' he says, pulling back his shorts to reveal some serious-looking scar tissue.

'The worst thing was that before I went into the operating theatre I had a meeting with the surgeon and he warned me that this could be it – the end of my career. You lie down and before they cut you open the last thing you're thinking before you go to sleep is that you might never play football again. When you're 20 or 21, that's pretty hard to deal with but nothing prepares you for how hard it is to come back from those injuries. I was in pain for a long time. Just lying down was painful.

'I went to Lilleshall [the national sports centre in Shropshire] to focus on the work because when I was at Derby, with my team-mates, it was like all lads together and I wouldn't get anything done. So I shut myself away at Lilleshall. I'd go up there on Monday and stay till Friday because they'd have three people telling you what to do. I was going on ten-mile bike rides, getting on the rowing machine, building up the strength again.'

When Ramage did return to full fitness, the path to the Derby first-team was blocked by million-pound signings. 'Even when I did get on as a sub, I would be straight out again. It didn't seem to matter how well I did, the people ahead of me were costing that much money... I was coming home heartbroken. There were tears on a Saturday night, I can tell you.'

* * *

And that's how Ramage's move to Watford came about. At the end of January 1994, Watford visited the Baseball Ground and won 2-1. 'I think that's when Glenn Roeder noticed me because I was marking the little tyrant, Andy Hessenthaler. I tell you, has he got an engine, by the way! I used to call him the little German. Anyway, I did well against him, made him run about a bit. I don't think Glenn had seen anyone get the better of Hessy like that.

'I knew I needed to get away from Derby. I'd put in three transfer requests while Arthur Cox was manager but he wouldn't let me go. Then Roy McFarland took over and eventually he accepted that I had to go. But after almost two years out of the game, you get forgotten.

'One day the phone at home went and it was Glenn. I'll never forget it because my missus, Amanda, asked who it was and I mouthed, "Glenn Roeder." She said, "Where?" So I mouthed, "Watford." And she went, "Oh."'

It wasn't a ringing endorsement then. 'No, not really,' Ramage laughs. 'I think she was more worried about the travelling. She was very close to her mum and dad and I knew she wouldn't want to move.'

Within a few weeks, Watford and Derby were due to meet again, this time at Vicarage Road. 'Roy Mac rang up and said, "I know you've been speaking to Glenn so I don't think it'd be right for you to come down. You won't be playing anyway, but I don't think it'd be right for you to travel with us either." So I knew the deal was close to getting done between the two clubs so I went down with my dad. Watford gave us some tickets and me and me old man wandered down. As soon as I got into Occupation Road I liked the vibe. I felt at home. I made up me mind that I'd sign.

'We watched the game and I think Marco Gabbiadini scored the winner for Derby right near the end. We lost 4-3 anyway.'

We? You'd not even signed the contract.

'I know! I was spewing, I tell you,' he laughs. 'That's how I knew it was the right team to join. I felt it straight away.

'I went to meet Glenn at the Hilton hotel in Watford and almost the first thing I said to him was, "I'm using this as a stepping stone." I think he quite liked that because he knew I was coming to Watford to do well.'

Ramage was the first of a number of new arrivals in spring 1994. Colin Foster and Keith Millen added steel to the defence and Tommy Mooney established himself as a crowd favourite immediately. I suggest to Ramage that he was something of a luxury player in a Watford team that struggled to elevate itself above the functional.

'Yeah, definitely,' he says. 'Glenn told the rest of the team that, too. He told the midfielders to get me the ball and he let me have that role just behind the front two. It's what every player dreams of.

'Glenn gave me a bit of freedom on and off the pitch. I lived in a hotel for my first year at Watford, then I lived with David Barnes, but Glenn would let me have Mondays off so I could spend a bit of time at home. I'd get straight on the M1 after a game and get home to the missus, have Sunday and Monday at home and then come back down to Watford.

'I was living in the Jarvis hotel on the A41 – you know, the one that's cheaper than the Hilton. It's hard work living in a hotel. There's nothing to do. I used to go up to Bushey, go to the bookies or the fry-up place next door and chat to the old fellas in there but it was difficult. I did get homesick because I was away from my friends and family.

'I used to go out with David Barnes for a few beers and Glenn wouldn't come down too hard on us because he knew I was away from home. He'd let us go out and then he'd take us for a long run round the woods to sweat out the beer. He knew all the tricks. If you'd had a heavy night the trick was to put a clove of garlic in your mouth to mask the smell.

'I played some of my best football at Watford, particularly in that first full season, so going out and having a few drinks once a week wasn't doing any harm. I was always professional; I never went out the night before a game.

'I remember one day Glenn took me and Barnesy out for a four-mile run and we got back into Vicarage Road, down the steps, into the players' tunnel and round the pitch and we were just finishing up, when wallop, I threw up all over the seats in the east stand. Glenn said: "Well, it's pretty obvious what you were doing last night." I nearly made it back to the dressing room, where I could have done it in the toilet, but no, all over the seats!'

* * *

Watford managed to avoid relegation but the following season did not start well and it looked like another scrap was ahead of them. Paul Furlong, top scorer for the previous two seasons, had been sold to Chelsea for £2.3m and his replacement, Jamie Moralee, struggled. Kevin Miller filled the space between the posts more imposingly than his immediate predecessors Simon Sheppard, Perry Digweed or Perry Suckling. Derek Payne added a certain unconventional graft in midfield. But it's fair to say that Roeder's team was defensive, which is perhaps not surprising considering he was a defender.

They lost 3-0 at Sheffield United on the opening day. 'It was a red hot day, that, wasn't it?' says Ramage. 'I didn't like playing in the sun. My tongue was hanging out when it was hot. Wait till it gets a bit colder and then, around Christmas time, I was firing.'

Watford won just two of their opening 11 league games – one of which was thanks to Richard Johnson's late thunderbolt against Graham Taylor's Wolves. But they lost 4-2 at home to Luton, 3-0 at Charlton and struggled to goalless draws against Grimsby and Barnsley. 'We were coming in and thinking, "Jesus, how have we lost that?" We played some good stuff but we weren't getting the results. And then it just clicked.'

Ramage's memory is perhaps being a little generous to his former team-mates there. That autumn was not one lifted by free-flowing football. Watford were, generally speaking, a team that created few chances. However, Ramage was at the centre of so much of the positive things Watford did. When he was firing, Watford were firing. The problem for the team was the lack of goals. Moralee, the summer's most expensive signing – £450,000 from Millwall – had not settled.

'Jamie was my mucker,' says Ramage. 'He was a lovely lad – a typical south London lad. He was my room-mate on away trips and he was a real Jack-the-lad but he was brilliant in the dressing room. He was always smiling, cracking jokes and he had all the chat. He's an agent now, isn't he? That job must suit him perfectly.

'I felt really sorry for him because he did work his socks off. He made all the runs, got in good positions but he just didn't get on a run of goals. He took a while to score and the crowd didn't really accept him. You could see his confidence sort of drain away and he never really recovered from that, did he?

'Jamie was really into his greyhound racing and a real gambling man. A few of us bought into this dog that the groundsman, Les Simmons, was training. I think it was me, Jamie, Payney [Derek Payne]. This dog cost me a fortune but we went to visit it and we thought it was the next big thing. We went to Walthamstow and we all lumped on it. Les told us it was flying so I stuck £250 on and it came nowhere. I don't think I'd ever had a bet before I came to Watford but I got in with the crowd that played cards. Here's a tip: don't play cards with Dave Holdsworth – Dodge, as we called him – because he's always got something up his sleeve. Pulling cards from everywhere, he was.

'We had some great characters at the time. Tommy Mooney would run through walls for the team. Payney was the scruffiest bloke you've ever seen. He'd come in with one red sock and one black sock on like he'd got dressed in the dark. There was always a laugh and a joke going on.'

After the New Year, Watford set a new club record for consecutive clean sheets – nine in the league and FA Cup – and that solid defence, coupled with the creativity Ramage and others brought to it, took Watford to an unlikely seventh place. They really were just a goalscorer away from the play-offs.

The final game of the season – arguably the best and most consistent season of Ramage's career – came against his old club, Derby, at Vicarage Road. 'Earlier in the season I'd won a penalty against my old mate Paul Williams in the game at the Baseball Ground, and in the *Derby Telegraph* before the game at Watford, their manager said something like, "We've got to be careful near Ramage when he gets in the box because he will go down."

'Anyway, I won another penalty against Jossie [Paul Williams] and Kevin Phillips missed it. Later in the game Hessy went down and we had an argument about who was going to take it. Hessy wanted Kev to take it but I grabbed the ball and scored it and we won 2-1. That was a nice way to finish the season.'

\* \* \*

Ramage and Roeder had a topsy-turvy relationship. The manager would give his most gifted player a bit of leeway and Ramage would take advantage. Over the summer, Ramage let his hair down.

'I'd had a good season. I'd been top scorer and we weren't far away from the play-offs so I was determined to have a good summer,' Ramage says. 'I'd been away from the missus so much, travelling up and down the motorway, so we had a couple of good holidays and before I knew it, the summer was gone. I managed to do a bit of running a week before we went back for pre-season training but you can't get a lot done in a week, so I probably was a bit overweight.

'We all had to get on the scales when we reported back and Glenn looked at me and said, "Are you sure this shirt's big enough for you?" I was probably only a stone over and I knew I'd lose it during pre-season training. While we were in Sweden we were warming up before a session and I was taking the mickey out of something and Glenn just lost it. He said to the other lads, "Sort him out, will you?"

'I got the weight off before the end of pre-season but in the final session before the first game of the season, Glenn chucked me a bib and made me stand in the wall while the first team pinged free-kicks around me. I was fuming after that because it means you're not playing in the game on Saturday. I banged on his door and asked what was going on. He said I wasn't fit but I was back down to my fighting weight.

'Glenn then told the media that I was overweight, which wasn't really on because I'd got the weight off by then.

'We played Sheffield United at home on the opening day and Payney scored the winner with an overhead kick and I thought, "Shit, I might struggle to get back in the team here." Glenn kept leaving me out of the team and the fans were asking me why I wasn't playing. I think they lost three in a row and the third game was Charlton away and I was at home. I didn't even travel with the squad. I was like a bear with a sore head when I wasn't playing…'

Ramage is interrupted by a shout from the kitchen.

'I can vouch for that,' says Amanda.

Ramage laughs and carries on with his story.

'So, we're playing Charlton away and I'm upstairs in the bath, listening to the football on the radio. I shouted down to her, "There's another one gone in, duck." Let me tell you, all this about players being gutted when their team loses when they're left out is bullshit. You want to be in that team. If we went on a 10-game unbeaten run I wasn't going to get back in, was I?

'Anyway, I walked in to training after they'd lost at Charlton and Jamie says, "You won't believe what the fans were singing on Saturday… 'Where's the Ramage gone? Where's the Ramage gone?'" So we start training and Glenn calls me over. I go over and he starts making this sniffing noise. "Can you smell that, son?" he said. "That's humble pie," he said. "Are you ready to get your season started? You're playing on Saturday." Fair play to Glenn – he's a nice fella. We had a few ding-dongs but I always respected Glenn.

Ramage's first game of the season was at Grimsby and he remembers a Watford fan throwing a pie at him when he ran over to take a corner. 'I think I bent down and pretended to take a bite out of it,' he says. In the next match, at home to Stoke, Ramage won a penalty after taking the ball into the area, pushing it a bit too far and – how can we put this? – diving. Ramage laughs. 'Yeah, it was a bit of dive that one. He [the Stoke defender] stuck his leg out – nowhere near me – and I just fell over. The Stoke player was chasing me around after that, calling me a cheating bastard. It was a bit hideous that one because he was nowhere near me.' Justice was done, in a way, because Kevin Phillips missed the penalty but Ramage was back. He scored twice: one of them a header, the other a curling free kick from the edge of the box. After his first goal he ran towards the Watford fans, lifted his shirt and patted his stomach.

'I used to love all that,' he says. 'I dragged the fans in. I let them get to know me a bit, even if it was just by giving them a crafty wink when I was taking a corner, or pretending to smoke a fat cigar after a goal. I think that's why they took to me. I was always waiting for them to start singing the old "One Craig Ramage." I didn't like it if someone else got a louder chant!'

* * *

The team had its swaggering talisman again but his form was not as good as the previous year and the team had deteriorated.

Results were poor and by the start of 1996 a bad start had turned into another full-blown relegation battle. 'I had a couple of niggling injuries and the pressure started building. It was not a very happy place to be,' Ramage says. 'When we were losing, I used to take it very hard. I'd be awake at night thinking about a chance I'd missed or whatever. It must have been terrible for Glenn because things weren't getting any better.'

Roeder was sacked in February, with Watford bottom of the First Division, seven points from safety. They needed a miracle.

'We didn't get to say our goodbyes,' says Ramage. 'He just went, which was a bit sad. Usually you get to shake the manager's hand and say thanks. I liked Glenn. He took a chance on me. I had one of my best years at Watford, I stayed injury free and I liked him.

'When Glenn had his brain tumour, I wrote a letter to him because I wanted to tell him what he meant to me. We were close but I probably did say a few harsh things to him here and there.

'Then we've got Graham Taylor coming home. Graham was England manager when I got my first under-21 cap so he obviously knew a bit about me as a young lad but I was a bit apprehensive. I'd heard he made you work your socks off, I knew the stories about the long-ball and I was worried he might not like the way I played.

'Graham came in and changed it around immediately. As a coach, Graham is one of the best managers I've ever worked with. When you work with him, you know he's not a long-ball merchant. He wanted the ball in the danger areas but he didn't mind you moving it around as long as everything was done quickly and you put it in where it's going to hurt the opposition. His coaching sessions were brilliant – he'd have us in stitches.'

Ramage was no longer the focal point of the midfield. Instead, Taylor pushed Ramage further forward. He scored twice in a 2-1 win over Oldham – Taylor's first victory since returning – and another two in the exhilarating 4-4 draw at West Bromwich Albion.

After a 1-1 draw at Southend United on Easter Monday, and with just six games remaining, Watford were still deep in trouble. In fact, relegation now looked inevitable because they were six points adrift of the next team, Luton Town. It was then that Taylor went for broke.

'He put me up front. We played with about five forwards, didn't we?' says Ramage.

Taylor used Devon White, Kerry Dixon, David Connolly and Ramage up front, with Mooney also getting forward. They beat Port Vale 5-2, Reading 4-2 and Port Vale 6-3 in consecutive home games. 'I couldn't hit a barn door before but once Graham came in, I started banging them in,' Ramage says, who scored 11 in the final 13 games of the season, including a hat-trick against Port Vale. 'Tommy Mooney tried to nick one of my goals in that one. I knocked it in and he tried to get the last touch with a backheel on the line and he ran off claiming it. I ran after him and said: "Oh no you don't, that's mine." It was amazing, frightening almost, because we had this momentum. Suddenly we had a lifeline and we went to Norwich and won and gave ourselves a chance of staying up on the final day. We had to beat Leicester. I was clean through after about five minutes and skied it over the bar.'

Watford lost but even victory would not have been enough. They were relegated, Graham Taylor moved 'upstairs' and Kenny Jackett took over as first-team manager.

'I was gutted when we went down, no word of a lie,' says Ramage. 'I didn't fancy playing in that league, and why should I? I'd scored goals in the First Division. I must be the only player to score 11 in 13 in that division and not be able to get a move. Don't get me wrong, I didn't want to leave Watford but they didn't offer me a contract. I was on a week-to-week. I wasn't on big money – about £900 a week. That's nowt, is it? There were players at Watford on a lot more than me. I didn't hold them to ransom; I didn't go in and say, "I want this money," but they didn't get me in either and make me an offer. They let Hessenthaler go, which I couldn't understand, but this is what Kenny Jackett does, let's some big characters go.

'I could have gone earlier. When Glenn was manager, Barry Fry came in for me and I was going to go to Birmingham. Glenn said: "Barry is taking the piss, trying to get you for nothing, but he might come in with more." Another time, I went and trained at Stoke because they were going to buy me and Glenn told me I had to keep it hush-hush. I was up there and their gaffer said: "We like you but how come you can do all the running when we're going forward but you don't like doing it the other way?" That was a bit of a worry. We had this training session where we were just running round and round the pitch all afternoon and as Mike Sheron came past me he said: "This club ain't for you, Rammo!" People reckoned I was brilliant going forward but not so good charging back. I don't know where that idea's come from! I had runners around me, didn't I? That's what it's all about. Let me do my thing and others can do their thing.

'That move came to nothing anyway because it ended up in the paper that I was talking to Stoke and Glenn rang me up saying: "You've let the cat out of the bag. The fans are going to go ape here!" So I went back to Watford. So I could have moved but I stayed because I liked it at Watford. It's just I wasn't sure I was going to fit into Kenny's team. I maybe wasn't what he was looking for.'

Fate intervened. After a couple of appearances at the start

of the 1996-97 season, Ramage came off the bench in a home game against Peterborough. 'I went up for a header, landed and the bones in my leg have hit each other because obviously I've got a bit of movement in my knee. I had a hairline fracture of my femur and tore my cartilage and that was me out for six months,' he says.

While he was recovering, the team was crying out for the Ramage of old. When he eventually got fit, Jackett sent him to Peterborough on loan. 'Barry Fry was the manager and they were making a documentary about him. Payney was there too. On the first day Barry said to me, "Rammo, you're on free-kicks, corners, penalties." It was a real eye-opener there, for sure. I was in the dressing room at half-time during my first game, steam coming off me because I'm breathing out my arse a bit, and the next thing I know Barry's tried to nut the left-back because he wasn't marking up at a corner. Then he said to the centre back, "You've cost me 25 goals this season." And the centre-back chucks orange juice in Barry's face and everyone's up on their feet trying to drag them apart. I thought, 'Bloody hell – what have I got into here?' But I really enjoyed my month there in the end.'

Ramage returned to Watford, got back into a team that was huffing, puffing and losing ground in the race for the play-offs, and scored twice in a 4-0 win against York that didn't so much offer hope as prolong the agony.

His last game for Watford at Vicarage Road ended prematurely when he was sent off against Chesterfield. 'My head went a little bit,' he says. 'It was the frustration of the whole season. Their centre half cracked me in the mouth and split my lip and I said, "That's how you want to play, is it?" A little bit later, Darren Bazeley hung up this beautiful cross and I just put my arm out and let him nut my elbow. There was a bit of a scuffle and I said, "That's 1-1, now, shall we leave it at that?" He spat blood in my face so the next time I gave him the old nutmeg, put the ball through his legs and ran past and he just pulled me back. The ref didn't give it, so I grabbed the fella round the throat and got the red card.'

* * *

'Graham Taylor pulled me in and said, "Look, why don't you go and get your career back on track?" That's the kind of man he was. He used the softly-softly approach and gave me a free transfer. I was going to go to Stoke but then Chris Kamara, the Bradford manager, said: "Don't do anything until I've spoken to you."

'I signed for Bradford and after Kammy got sacked, Paul Jewell came in and we made it to the Premier League. One of our first games was away at Watford and I was on the bench. 'Graham came and gave me a big hug before he shook Paul Jewell's hand. I think Graham liked me in his own little way.'

After Bradford, he went to China to play for a team in Xaopyangon managed by Paul Rideout. He lasted three days. 'They offered good money – £75,000 tax free for five months – but that way of life wasn't for me. We were in a restaurant and they pointed at this tank of bullfrogs and they asked me which one I wanted to eat. I was only there three days and I must've lost a stone.'

As soon as he got home, he signed for Notts County but his career ended when a compression treatment went wrong. 'It's like a balloon and it covers you from the top of your leg to your toes. They fill it with ice and it repairs your muscles but a piece of ice got trapped against my peroneal nerve. At first it felt like when you sleep on your arm, so I had a hot bath, but it didn't get better. It was like it was dead.

'The next morning, I woke up and looked down on my silk

sheets – my Del Boy sheets – and I couldn't lift my ankle. My brain was telling my foot to move and it wouldn't move.

'For four years I was paralysed from the knee down and for a while I didn't know if it would ever get back to normal. I was sort of dragging my foot around. I've got back to 95 per cent movement now but it was scary.'

Ramage is reluctant to talk too much about the incident, for legal reasons, but explains that he was compensated from the club's insurance policy when he was forced to retire.

He began another lengthy rehabilitation process and had to work out what he was going to do next. 'The first few months were okay but then suddenly it hit me and I was in a dark place for a while,' he says. 'I was 31. All I'd done my whole life was play football. I couldn't do any coaching work because of my foot and I wondered what I was going to do. In my head, I was going to carry on until I was 35 so in a way I wasn't prepared.

'My injuries killed me really. I played 250 games and scored 50 goals which, considering the injuries, I don't think is too bad. I do wonder what would have happened if I'd not had those injuries, though.

'I wasn't a millionaire. I didn't play football for money anyway. I just wanted a nice house and a car and that would do me. I'd paid my house off, which not many people could say at my age, but you're a long time retired.

'Footballers are like big kids, really. You never really grow up. Everything is looked after for you. It can be a big shock going out into the big bad world.

'I knew I had to work so I qualified as a digger driver. I was driving nine-tonne diggers, working on the flood defences in Nottingham for a friend of mine. I could take a millimetre of your lawn with a digger if you needed me to. I went out and earned a living because I had to but, yeah, there were some dark days.'

Ramage became a father for the first time in his early forties. 'She's the best thing I've ever done, I swear. Mandy lost her parents and then a little one comes along and it changes everything. It takes ten years off you being an older parent. Well, it puts ten years on and takes ten off!

'My daughter is everything to us. I just wish I'd had her when I was 21.'

Getting back involved in football through his commentary work for BBC Three Counties and BBC Derby has given Ramage a way to reconnect with the game. 'I love it,' he says. 'I love the guys I work with and I call it how I see it because I think that's what the fans want to hear.

'I've had a couple of good years doing it, although so far I've seen Watford lose a play-off final at Wembley, and then Derby lose a play-off final at Wembley. That's got to change soon. Maybe one can go up automatically and the other can go up at Wembley.'

You don't fancy a Watford versus Derby play-off final then, Craig?

'I don't think the nerves would take it. But then again, I couldn't lose, could I?'

# AIDY BOOTHROYD

**On joining Watford**

'One of the promises I made to the players was telling them that I was going to push them beyond what they thought they could do.'

# 4

Aidy Boothroyd is one of only two men to lead Watford to the top flight.

But when he was unveiled as the club's new manager in March 2005, most people wondered, Adrian who?

However, his confidence more than made up for his lack of experience and 14 months later he led the Hornets to the Premier League.

For a while it seemed that everything he touched turned to gold but eventually the magic wore off.

These days, Boothroyd cuts a far humbler figure than the man who thought he could do no wrong. Here, we find him in reflective mood...

# AIDY BOOTHROYD

It doesn't quite warrant a commemorative T-shirt, but I was there when Aidy Boothroyd, or Adrian as he was then, was presented to the media as the new Watford manager at Vicarage Road. The date was Tuesday March 29, 2005, and I had been reporting on the story for *Sky Sports News* ever since Ray Lewington had been sacked the week before. It followed a 2-0 home defeat to Preston – the fourth loss in five matches.

Finding out that Lewington had been dismissed was a memorable experience in itself. I recall a member of staff at Vicarage Road calling me, clearly distressed, saying, 'Ray's gone – he's been sacked!' while choking back the tears.

I spent the intervening week, which was fixture-less due to international matches, on the phone to a range of characters all with differing emotions. Lewington was understandably down-beat and disillusioned. Graham Simpson, the chairman, was a mixture of cautiousness and dogged optimism, while chief executive Mark Ashton was guarded and confident that the right man would be found.

Prospective candidates were spoken to throughout the week. Are you interested? Have you had an interview? I asked eagerly. The majority, including Luther Blissett, reflected a resigned acknowledgement that, as with many appointments in football, someone was already nailed on for the role.

Boothroyd's name came up early in conversations with sources at Watford and in Leeds. It seemed certain, albeit slightly disconcerting at a crucial time of the season, that a curve ball appointment was in the offing and Boothroyd was on a golden path to the golden boys despite being unknown.

It wasn't until the morning of the press conference that I was finally able to confirm his appointment. I remember sitting on my car bonnet as I broke the news to *Sky Sports News* viewers, while reading sketchy information about this untried and untested 34-year-old from my notepad. It is fair to say that Adrian Boothroyd was not a big-name appointment.

After the press conference I had the opportunity to do the first one-on-one TV interview with the new boss. I warmed to him from the beginning. He accepted that he was a novice and was a risk but he exuded an air of confidence that belied his inexperience. I found that an impressive trait and, not simply because I was a Watford fan, I wanted him to succeed.

The main thing I took away from that day was, in fact, something tangible that has lasted the test of time. It was the nametag that was placed on the top table for that first press conference as he launched himself into the public domain. Quite why I decided that a flimsy folded piece of A4 paper with his name and a club badge on would be worth keeping is beyond me but I still have it in a drawer somewhere.

It now serves to symbolise his humble beginning. The foundations of Boothroyd's managerial career were paper thin.

From there he would go on to write one of the most significant chapters in the club's history, becoming only the second Watford manager to win promotion to the top division. There would be plenty of fanfare and career-defining football, while ego, controversy and mistakes would also feature along the way.

This interview tackles some of the key events of his reign – from his unexpected arrival and success at the club, his unconventional methods on and off the field and in the transfer market, his fractious departure and his decision to go back to the drawing board as he battled to rekindle a career that had started with such a buzz.

### When did you first know you had a chance of getting the Watford manager's job?

When Ray Lewington got the sack, I phoned up Mark Ashton and said, 'I would love to have a crack at this.' He said, 'I can get you an interview because I've pushed for you, but I can't do anything other than that.' It was already a pretty big thing to be able to do but he'd got me through the door, no doubt about that. I wouldn't say we were massive mates but we had a good working relationship, we trusted and enjoyed working with one another. *[The pair had worked together at West Bromwich Albion, where Boothroyd had been youth development manager.]*

In the interview, everything that could have gone right, went right. I was in full flow, I was 'at it' and I came away thinking I'd done as well as I could. I was one of five or six that got cut down to two, the other being Colin Calderwood.

I had to convince them because Graham Simpson and the Russo brothers weren't stupid people. I got invited back for a second interview, which was much more informal. I knew that I was their favourite from the start, but because I had absolutely no experience at it, I think they thought, 'Christ! We better get him back just to double-check.'

In the end I got it and I thought, 'Fucking hell! Brilliant!'

### What was your overriding emotion being introduced for the first time as the Watford manager in March 2005?

I felt daunted. I think anyone that doesn't feel self-doubt at some point is lying. We all have our little dark moments, but I knew where I wanted to be and I knew what I wanted to do and I had the energy and enthusiasm. And regarding set-backs, shit happens – it's just about getting on with it.

**Did you feel you had to be extra positive from the start in front of the cameras because of your inexperience?**

This is not an act – this is who I am. I am a bit naughty with some of the things I say some of the time, and I do go close to the edge with people, but I'm not putting on an act. This is who I am.

It wasn't difficult because I did believe, and I knew we could achieve things. But I knew that if I wasn't positive then how were the players and fans going to believe that we could do it? The manager sets the tone in a place and I knew if I could get them to believe in me then I could get them to do things.

The only thing I will say about the media is that I milked it for all that it was worth. If there was the chance to do an interview, I would be at the opening of an envelope, to the point that by the end of that season I was absolutely drained from all the highs and lows of it, but I knew I had to establish myself.

**What did you say to the players when you first met them at the training ground after your appointment?**

I just sat in front of them and knew that I couldn't give any Churchillian speeches because some of those players didn't even know who I was. I knew they weren't stupid – I knew they'd speak to their mates at Leeds to find out about me.

I said: 'I promise you that I'll push you. I know some of you are older than me but that's fine; I'll always treat you with respect. But when I ask you to work, I want you to do what I want you to do.' I wasn't too high and wasn't too low, and then we went to go and train.

One of the promises I made to the players was telling them that I was going to push them beyond what they thought they could do.

I said: 'If I have a go at you, I'm doing it for you, but

believe me I will have a go at you if you don't toe the line.'

All those lads, if ever I can help them now, I will, because I know that they have done great for me.

**You were in charge for seven games at the end of the 2004-05 season and finished two points clear of relegation. You then targeted promotion the next campaign – and created a 'bus' with the chairs in the meeting room at the training ground to get everyone heading in the same direction. Explain.**

I did lay out the chairs like they are on a bus. I put them together with one at the front for the driver. I wanted it to be a metaphor for what we wanted to do. I told them we were aiming for automatic promotion – play-offs as a minimum. I said: 'This is the bus and I want you to come and sit on the bus.' I remember Paul Devlin looking at me, then looking at the lads and thinking: 'Is he sure?'

If you don't set a target for people, how do they know if they can achieve it? I was initially sitting facing the way the driver would face, but then I turned to face them and explained what I wanted from them.

**What were the foundations for success that season?**

The pillars were the players and the staff. We had a very good, open learning environment. We had strong characters like Marlon King, Gavin Mahon and Malky Mackay who were big influences in the group. We also had lots of young players, but also some players in the middle of their careers who'd lost their way a bit – Clarke Carlisle, Matthew Spring, Paul Devlin, Chris Eagles and Jordan Stewart – and they fitted into the system and they worked hard and fought for each other. The players had a belief that we could beat anyone. We had a target of 84 points and we got 81.

It was exciting, it fizzed. Some of the nights we had there, beating QPR at home and beating Norwich away, we just didn't give up. I think that our supporters and people in general respected that. I think they liked what we were doing because we were underdogs and I was a rookie manager and I was being outspoken about a few things, and I was very confident because I knew what I was doing and I knew where I wanted them to be.

No disrespect to Ray Lewington before me, but sometimes things work in cycles and there needs to be a clean break so you can go again with a new group. The same then happened when Brendan Rodgers took over from me and then Malky and Sean Dyche got it going again.

**Ultimately that first full season went to plan, but what challenges did you face?**

I decided to play teams in pre-season that we could beat to simply get the confidence going. Then we came up against Preston on the opening day and got beat 2-1 but it could have been six. So I said, 'You have a choice here, Aidy: you can either play the way that you want to play and be happy with yourself going home or you can make a real go of this, be clever and play in a way that suits your players and bring in players that you know you can entice.'

There had been a couple of bad buys like Sietes, who I brought in because I wanted to play a certain way, but who didn't play once. Christ! What a bad buy he was. He was hopeless – absolutely hopeless. I very quickly thought, 'What the fuck are you doing? He can't do it.' I brought in the likes of Martin Devaney and a few others that could play but weren't quite up to the level.

To be fair I had no idea about recruitment and scouting and I would go blind on players on the advice of others within my staff. When you're a rookie, you don't realise until you've done it that you're making mistakes.

Now this is where I look back, now that I'm a little bit

older and wiser, and realise I got great support from the
board, Simpson and the Russo brothers. I remember going
into a board meeting and saying, 'I've made a right mistake
with Sietes,' and they paid him up within about six weeks.
Now that is proper faith in your manager.

But then, thankfully and very quickly, Ben Foster, Malky,
Jordan and Matthew arrived, and Marlon made a massive
difference for us. All of a sudden I'd gone from three or four
absolute nightmare buys to really good ones. Then we got on
a roll. And because I was disciplined with them and because
I pushed them, the environment was good for learning. We
were doing debriefs after games before a lot of people started
doing that, we were pushing boundaries because of the staff
that we assembled and we were also able to keep the players
really fit due to the medical and sports science staff.

We just blitzed it and went on a proper run and picked up
belief along the way. Every so often we'd get a beating and
lose by three or four goals, like at Coventry or Burnley, but
we'd just bounce back straight away. It wasn't until we lost to
Millwall and Palace in March that we lost games back to back.

I was having the time of my life, but I'd already learned
lessons about recruitment and on the style of play.

I'm not a man who is all about the long ball. I've always
believed that you have to attack in a variety of ways and you
have to be able to mix it up. But only a fool plays in a way that
doesn't suit the players that he's got, because there is only one
way that he's going and that is out the door.

I almost seem apologetic for it, but I'm not. I don't
apologise for being successful and doing what I did with what
I had. And generally you find that people will throw stones
when you beat them. I remember a couple of managers
saying that it wasn't the right way to play. Well, it's easy for a
manager to say that about you when he's just been beaten 4-1,

so I didn't pay too much attention.

The football we played in the first season was vibrant, fantastic, attacking and very bold, but we played to our strengths. Darius Henderson and Marlon were two very good front men – strong, quick and direct.

People can't tell me that Ashley Young and Matthew Spring are direct players, because they're not. We played in a variety of ways and one thing we were especially good at was counter-attacking. We entertained, we won and we scored goals. Over 80 that season.

**The season ended with victory over Leeds, where you'd worked previously, in the play-off final in Cardiff. How vital was 'inside knowledge' and detailed preparation?**
I knew all of the Leeds players because I'd been there a year earlier. I knew the environment and I knew the situation that Kevin Blackwell was in with the board. It was basically a house of cards. Even though they had good players, there was a lot going on behind the scenes that was a nightmare for the manager.

I felt that we were stronger people and characters, and as a team we were more united than they were. I would go to war with my players and they felt the same about me. You just feel it; sometimes you know it's your time.

I spoke to Dave Bassett. I spoke to Sir Clive Woodward about practising penalties, which we did against Ipswich in the penultimate home game of the regular season. It was brilliant and worked out really well for the crowd especially.

We went down early to Cardiff and stayed in St David's Bay. We went to the stadium, took a ball on the pitch and I wanted the media to know what we were doing because I wanted Kevin to know. I also knew that the Leeds players' wives were having to pay for themselves.

Ken Bates tried to pay more than us to get into the Vale

of Glamorgan, but the hotel stuck with us because we had booked it first. Then the chairman said that the club would pay for all the wives to go down. So my wife, Emma, took all the WAGS down to Cardiff on the Friday, then went off to a show or something in town while we prepared as per usual. The players knew that everything was being looked after.

We practised how we were going to act in the tunnel, how you stand, how you look at people and how you can intimidate people. Sometimes that works and sometimes it doesn't but thankfully it did. We all believed that it was our time and we believed we were going to win it.

**Following promotion, and just eight games into the Premier League season, your top scorer Marlon King was ruled out for six months with injury. How did that impact on Watford's chances of staying in the division?**
I'd never been in the Premier League before, I didn't really know how to use the transfer windows and I should have got another striker in the summer but I didn't. Marlon's injury really gave us problems. We knew he could score goals in the Premier League but when we lost him we had to play differently. We had Darius Henderson up front and we had to play to his strengths, and we became more direct as a team. We were almost playing like Norway with Tore Andre Flo, where we'd try to hit him and then play off the bits, because we thought that if we played football against these teams we'd get battered.

We tried to be impressive with set plays. We tried to be aggressive and work harder than the opposition, and often for 75 minutes we did, but the quality and depth invariably told.

The way that the media is, and the way that the Premier League was viewed, meant more scrutiny. I remember a journalist coming up to me after we'd lost against Sheffield United at home in the last minute and saying that it was the

worst Premier League game he'd ever seen. I couldn't argue
with him because he was right – it was – but what was I
supposed to do? We could have changed it and maybe gone
down the Ian Holloway route from when he was in charge at
Blackpool and been super open. Maybe that would have been
a better thing for me personally in terms of my reputation.

As time went on, we used players like Hameur Bouazza
more and, along with Ashley Young, we tried to play more
open football. But as with any good players, when they do well
they get moved on. I wouldn't criticise the chairman at the
time because I also felt that it was the right thing to do. *[Young
joined Aston Villa, Bouazza went to Fulham.]* Getting £9m for
Ashley – a player that we'd brought through from the youth
team – was good business. We had to do it.

**If that was good business, signing Nathan Ellington,
who cost £3.25million and scored five goals in 56 games
for the club over a four-year period, could be described as
catastrophic business. That became part of your legacy.
Is that fair?**

Yes, without a doubt. The chairman backed me when we
knew Marlon was going to leave the next season and we
needed a replacement. Nathan had been brilliant at Wigan and
Bristol Rovers. He was a handful, he could run and he could
score. We'd analysed his goals, he'd score left foot, right foot,
headers, he was just a fantastic goalscorer. However, he was in
a period of his life where he'd just got married, he'd changed
his religion and he'd lost his way a little bit at West Brom and
me being me thought, 'I can get this kid going again.' But I
couldn't do it. It got to the point where I was thinking, 'C'mon
Nath, C'mon.' If I could have my time over again, I would
never have got him, but at the time it seemed like exactly the
right thing to do, because I felt I could turn him around. It
was a lesson learned, but a very, very painful one.

**In 2007-08, Watford were top of the Championship after 32 games but then a run of only one win in the final 14 matches saw them sneak into the play-offs only on goal difference. What happened?**

Losing Adam Johnson in November didn't help. *[Johnson, who had been on loan, went back to Middlesbrough.]* Sometimes players give everyone a lift and he was one of those players. But we had players' contracts up and they were asking for money that they'd never had before. Would we have gone up if Adam had stayed? I'm pretty sure we would have, but would I have been as well-rounded a person as I am now? Probably not.

We were the hunter when we were promoted but all of a sudden we got a bit fat and happy. Sometimes you can be on the crest of a wave and then you hit a huge slump.

It was a tough time because we'd done all this brilliant work. We'd all created this fantastic team and I just saw it all falling apart. Although we had brought players in, we were there to be shot at now, and we hadn't had that before. After a great start, people kept on comparing us to Devon Loch.

**After defeat in the play-off semi-final against Hull, the following season would be your last. You were sacked after 15 league games following a breakdown in your relationship with chairman Graham Simpson and chief executive Mark Ashton. How do you feel about your final few months at Vicarage Road?**

It was a very difficult time because I was quite fractious and I was irritable because I didn't like the position we were in.

It goes in cycles and it's about growing up as a person. I wanted things my own way and I felt that having been promoted I should be able to get what I wanted, but that's a stupid young man's view on life. It isn't like that and that's a lesson that I have learned. One of the many great lessons that I have learned.

I think when you go from an £8million turnover to a £48m turnover like we did, there are going to be a lot of things that have to change. I didn't have much experience of the situations we were facing but I wanted players who had served us well to get rewarded. I got rewarded and we all got rewarded, because the money was there.

To be fair to Graham, he put his money where his mouth was during that promotion season, and put a lot of his own personal wealth on the line. I'd had a great relationship with both Graham and Mark. It was really strong and really tight, we'd worked really hard along with the rest of the staff and the majority of the time the atmosphere in the offices was vibrant. But the relationships did break down in the end although I wouldn't be able to blame Graham and Mark. I'm sure they would say that there are some things that they would have done differently. I certainly would.

We all played our part in how strong it was and we all played our part in how it all fell apart. Would I change it? Yeah, probably, but I'm sure I will bump into them at some point in the future and it'll all be fine because all I want to do now is focus on the positive stuff.

I haven't spoken to either of them since I left. I was simply told that that was going to be it. I did go back to see the players, but only briefly. I will never forget that they gave me the opportunity and I'm sure at some point our paths will cross again.

One thing I've always done, and always will do, is look in the mirror first, and if I'm out of order I will say so. I'll never forget Watford. It's helped shape who I am.

If there are people who don't think highly of me then it's simply the case that if you want to be successful then you're going to piss people off and you can't be liked by everybody. If you go through your life aiming to have everyone like you,

you're not going to be any good, but there is a correct way to be and maybe I wasn't at particular times, I fully admit that, I wouldn't deny that.

When I came back as manager of Coventry and I came out after the game and the fans gave me a great reception, it was one of the most overwhelming things I'd ever experienced. It was a relief, I guess, because I loved the time I had there – even the not-so-good stuff – for my growth as a person.

**You were replaced by Brendan Rodgers, who revealed in** *Tales from the Vicarage Volume One*, **that you had wanted to bring him in as coach alongside you. Did you feel betrayed when he got the job?**

We were big mates for a long time. I was at Peterborough when he was at Reading, then he was at Chelsea and we used to meet at coaching courses. I did indeed want to bring Brendan in at one point as a number two. I was also interested in bringing in Nigel Pearson at the time.

Then the next thing is I've left and Brendan has my old job and he's saying, 'The style of play is going to change,' and all that, which at the time I was quite angry about. But when I look back, when I took over from Ray Lewington I was probably saying many of the same things and it wasn't meant to be disrespectful to the previous manager.

I bumped into Brendan when he was manager of Swansea and I was manager of Coventry and I said a few words to him then. And we exchanged what we thought about the situation.

When I left Watford, I had a high opinion of myself. I was full of it and I got emotional and upset about things that nowadays wouldn't even touch the sides. I wouldn't be bothered about them as an older bloke. I was just a bit sensitive, I think, and I had a bit of an ego at the time to say the least. When I look back now I think, 'Brendan didn't fucking say anything out of order, he was only doing what every manager does when they go into a new club.' So over a period of time I thought, 'You're being a bit daft there Aid, relax a little bit.'

Then Brendan and I ended up climbing Kilimanjaro on an expedition for the Marie Curie charity and we were put in the same room, we sat next to each other on the flight and shared a tent together. We lived in each other's pockets. By spending time together I got to realise that he is a really good bloke. So now we're friends and there is absolutely no problem at all.

**You now have a role with the FA working with the under-20s. How do you feel about your career since being in charge at Vicarage Road?**

Right now I'm in the perfect place. It's actually really good. I've got a great job, just where I need to be now in my career after blasting onto the scene at Watford and getting some massive highs and success in three-and-a-half years there.

When I came out of Watford I had a lot of interviews with clubs like West Brom, Reading, Swansea and Norwich but didn't get them. So I took an opportunity at Colchester. Then I'm not sure whether the Northampton situation was brave or stupid.

After leaving there, I thought, 'I've got to be careful here, or else I could end up going down the vortex never to be seen again. I have to get something that's right for me where I can still grow and improve as a coach and a manager.' Then the England job came along and it was the most stringent interview I've ever had and I managed to get this job. Now I'm working with international players but I've obviously got a reputation and a stigma that I have to shake off.

**How do you go about changing the perception of your style of football in your current position and shake off the nickname the critics gave you of Aidy 'Hoofroyd'?**

I've come through that, and now I'm exactly where I want to

be and enjoying being a football coach again. I don't get upset about people calling me 'long ball' or 'Hoofroyd' or anything else any more. I used to. And I guess in the end at Watford I was irritated about that, and I tried to change the way we played and I didn't quite do it.

Now, if the England under-20s start banging it long then I suppose everyone will be happy. The proof will be in the pudding with me.

We're rewriting our England DNA now on how we're going to play, and what we're going to do, and it's an exciting time to be involved. What do my peers think? Well, I'm respected on the whole. There are a few that have a pop, but they don't know enough about me, so it doesn't upset me and I don't worry about it. In fact, I'm relishing the challenge because that is the sort of bloke I am.

All I would say is come and watch a training session and come and see what I do. Thankfully Gareth Southgate, Sir Trevor Brooking and Dan Ashworth have been brave enough to appoint me, so I don't have any fear because I know that I can do it.

What a lot of people don't understand when they say, 'What the hell is he doing working at the FA?' is that when I was working at Peterborough, Norwich and West Brom I actually wrote the technical programmes for those clubs and I used to work with the under-nines and tens about ball manipulation, on playing through the thirds of the pitch, on opening out and being creative. All of those things are things that I'm doing now.

Kids are coming through into the first teams and they need to know what it's like. My background is youth and bringing players through with the ball. I'm very grateful for what I've had so far and I'm not bitter and twisted one bit, because I've got some fantastic memories.

# PAUL FURLONG

**On leaving Watford**

'Bruce Dyer was the first to go and he kind of left me behind. I remember having a conversation with him and he was telling me that I could do it too.'

# 5

Football can teach every young fan about life, about loyalty and about coping with loss.

Everyone can remember the day their first favourite player left the club. The bewildering sense of being abandoned for something better can linger for a long time. Seeing your former idol in someone else's colours always stings.

Paul Furlong's departure to Chelsea in 1994 tested one young fan's loyalty to the limit...

## PAUL FURLONG

My parents knew I was going to be speaking to them. When I got home my dad was washing the dishes, and he said: 'What happened?'

'I've signed!' I said, and he just started crying. I'll never forget that. He was so emotional that his boy had got what he wanted. They were good times.

**Paul Furlong, 2014**

That same day in May 1994, a 14-year-old throws a copy of the *Evening Standard* onto the seat alongside him and walks from the grooved wooden floor of an underground train and steps onto the concrete platform. The guard's head then protrudes from the next door down as he walks past. He's now clutching the discarded paper, which highlights on the front page an in-depth piece on the new South Africa president, Nelson Mandela.

It was something that the boy hadn't noticed when it had been in his possession. He'd always start reading at the back of the paper and stop when it got to the small print of the horse racing results.

He heads up the hill away from the station and along the high street. He passes Our Price, where Wet Wet Wet's new one, *Love is All Around,* plays. It was being tipped for big things and would go straight in at the top of the charts later that week.

He's taken a slight detour so he can check out the new

7-Eleven convenience store on the corner on the way down to the park. With its floor-to-ceiling chiller cabinets and imported sweets it was as if little piece of Greenwich Village had been transported to London. He's been told the shop stocks Tab Clear, a soft drink that is apparently 'the future' and will render Coke obsolete.

The boy eventually makes it to his front door, feeling a slight cramp in his cheek as he gnaws through his third piece of bubble gum that came free with the 1994 World Cup stickers he's bought.

He'd yet to buy an album to put them in and was still unsure whether he'd bother, seeing as England had been pushed, pulled and flicked out of competing by the villainous Ronald Koeman, who he'd seen staring up at him from one of the packets when he removed the gum.

Then came the homecoming ritual. He walks straight down the hall into the living room, picks up the TV remote and goes through a process that was now automatic.

Press one for BBC1.

Press 'Text'.

Press the buttons 3 – 0 – 2 then wait for the numbers to tick round.

Sometimes Ceefax, the pre-internet internet, worked at a speed slower than dial-up.

While he waits, he glances at the date on the screen. It's Thursday May 26.

Then he has a shock. His face sets. It's as if Noel Edmonds has just shouted, 'Go!' and his own image has appeared on the television screen during the NTV feature on Noel's House Party, the staple of Saturday night telly.

Shock is an understatement. It feels like his heart has been ripped out of his chest. He's gobsmacked. Then, as the news washes over him, he feels crestfallen.

Under the blue and green heading on BBC Ceefax's Sport home page, there it is – the top story of the day – in large, blocky white letters on the black screen, changing everything.

**FURLONG SIGNS FOR CHELSEA     303**

This was how sports news broke in those days. A football team's season could be made or broken in little pixelated letters. And this latest development was about to push this boy's relationship with the club he loved to breaking point.

The news would take time to sink in fully but already he knew everything would be different from now on. Already he was contemplating drastic action. For Furlong, this was a dream transfer but for the boy it was his worst nightmare.

Ten years prior to the arrival of their billionaire owner Roman Abramovich, Chelsea sourced their wares from more humble origins. They shopped at C&A rather than Harrods. They were still rooting through the sale rails rather than getting their garments made to measure.

Chelsea had only spent £2million on a player once before. Their previous record signing was the striker Robert Fleck, who joined from Norwich the summer before and had flopped at Stamford Bridge.

Now Furlong had to deal with the heavy burden. He'd been Watford's top scorer during two unremarkable seasons in the second tier – they'd finished 16th and 19th – but Chelsea were prepared to break their transfer record, shelling out £2.3million.

Three summers earlier, Furlong had moved from non-league Enfield to top-flight Coventry City for £130,000. After one season, in which he scored four goals, he dropped down to Watford. Now, aged 25, he was returning to the Premiership for almost 20 times the figure the Sky Blues had paid.

'Something that I got into my head early doors was that the money was nothing to do with me,' says Furlong when we meet. 'That was something that two clubs had agreed was right in relation to my services. What I needed to do was get on the field and do what I did best, and most importantly try to improve my game at the highest level,' he says.

His journey to the top division had started from base camp. These days the story of Jamie Vardy's rise from non-league to Leicester City in the Premier League is treated as if it were a miracle, but back in the 1980s and 1990s top clubs were happy to take a punt on those playing semi-professionally. Ian Wright had made the transition from non-league to Crystal Palace and then Arsenal. Furlong had scored twice in Enfield's FA Trophy final replay victory over Telford United at The Hawthorns and had been capped by England's semi-pro team.

Like many at that level, Furlong happily combined a full-time job with non-league football, until he was made redundant as a driver for Ferodo delivering car parts. His manager at Enfield, Peter Taylor, suggested he go for a trial at Watford.

Taylor knew the Watford manager, Steve Perryman, from their playing days at Tottenham, and that paved the way.

At the end of a successful week-long trial, Furlong was told that Watford wanted to sign him the following Monday, once Perryman returned from the first team's away trip.

In the meantime, Furlong got a call from Coventry City's manager, Terry Butcher, who was able to offer Division One football. He invited Furlong up to the Midlands to meet him.

'I went up to see him on the Saturday morning and I liked what he had to say so I then ended up putting pen to paper with them,' says the former striker. 'It came to the Monday and I remember having to have a conversation with Steve but I don't remember there being too much hard feeling. I remember him wishing me well and telling me to go and enjoy my football.'

It later transpired that Perryman was having trouble convincing the club's owner, Jack Petchey, to gamble more than £100,000 on a non-league striker. As Perryman said, he could have saved Petchey a few quid because Watford signed Furlong a year later for £250,000.

That move came about when Coventry's new manager, Don Howe, decided Furlong was surplus to requirements. He left Highfield Road and began a two-year spell with the Hornets.

\* \* \*

Fast forward a couple of years and Furlong's departure had sparked feelings of loss, anger, solitude and desperation in our boy. The glory days of the 1980s seemed so long ago now and, besides, he'd been just a child when Watford rubbed shoulders with the giants of English football. The newly-formed Premier League seemed out of reach now the Sky had been lifted so high above their heads. Watford were fully signed-up members of the second tier, a sort of waiting room for the dreamers and the desperate.

Luther Blissett's departure – for the third and final time – in 1992 seemed to bring the curtain down on an era. Furlong arrived to lead the line, and quickly the boy took him into his heart. A strong, quick goalscoring centre forward easily catches the eye of a teenager looking for a hero. Furlong fitted the bill but what sort of reception would he get when he met his peers, the other players?

'The fact that I'd come from Coventry, from the old First Division, carried a bit of weight and I was accepted into the dressing room. I had no issues or no problems and I think these things are easily ironed out after the first training session where people can see whether you're a player or not,' says Furlong.

From training to competitive action, and six goals in his

first nine starts, albeit amidst just one win, helped convince not only his team-mates but the fans that Furlong could go the distance.

'It was an easy transition to go back to Watford and, looking back on it, it has made me the person I am today within the game because that is where I learned my trade under Steve Perryman and Kenny Jackett,' says Furlong. 'You knew what they wanted. Both of them were very professional, plain, simple and concise. It wasn't rocket science.'

\* \* \*

Back at school in the chemistry lab in May 1994, the boy would marvel – internally, at least, as it would be uncool to show genuine joy in a science lesson – at how magnesium and water would combust so violently when combined. Elsewhere in his mind, a similarly violent reaction was threatening to overcome his sensibilities as he contemplated the departure of Furlong.

A piercing light of uncertainty blinded him. How could it ever be the same again?

From a team perspective, Furlong's first season was unspectacular. Watford finished 16th in the table but the new striker had, by some distance, stood out, and he won the player of the year award. He'd scored 22 goals, 19 of them in the league. He'd made a crucial contribution as Watford kept themselves just above the snarling teeth and snapping jaws of the relegation dogfight, but the humble North Londoner was never one to get above his station.

'I loved the game and I knew that if I wasn't playing professionally I would still be playing on a Sunday morning for nothing, so to get paid for it was something that I didn't want to lose in a hurry,' says Furlong.

During the time that Furlong was at the club, our teenager

would wear his Watford shirt with pride at lunch breaks, when mass 20-a-side matches would break out on the pitches at his school. These were great days. His Arsenal, Tottenham and Manchester United-supporting mates would even toss him a compliment. 'That Furlong is a good player, isn't he?' Never before had any Watford player been noticed by his peers during his time at secondary school. Some of these Premier League supporters even fancied 'Furs' for their team.

Furlong, though, was not getting carried away.

'I was level-headed and I had a good family set-up around me that kept me grounded. I was never one to blow my own trumpet and I tried to keep things in perspective,' he says. 'I've worked with managers over the years who've looked for players that are on that happy medium, rather than too high when you're doing well or vice versa. So I just tried to keep steady and that's how I tried to conduct myself throughout life.'

There was nothing steady about how his number one fan was carrying himself at school. He was the first to talk up the qualities of Watford's top man in the competitive playground environment. For arguably the first time in his football-supporting life, he felt he had someone that he was proud to be associated with, and he wasn't going to waste the opportunity. He loved life while Furlong was banging in the goals at Vicarage Road. He was even enjoying his education, much like the man himself.

'Being raw, having come from non-league football and having never really having been taught where to make my runs, it was mainly just coming from instinct,' says Furlong about his style of play and eye for goal. 'I was fresh and needed coaching, and used to spend time with Kenny Jackett after training. He'd tell me where to make the runs and pick up my positions and I blossomed from that.'

Something else that soon came into bloom was Furlong's

relationship with his young strike partner Bruce Dyer. Furlong noticed his talent early on.

'I remember him being a youth team player when I was at the club and him coming over to train with us on occasion to come and get a feel for things,' recalls Furlong. 'I saw straight away that he had potential. He was quick and wiry. He not only ran with the ball but he recognised the times when he could pop it off and get the return pass. Looking back, I was right, and between the two of us we struck up a good partnership.'

Dyer would come off the bench twice in the last four games of the 1992-93 season. His debut against Birmingham came four days after his 18th birthday, although it was the following season when the two would successfully dovetail. 'He was quicker than me and more nimble and I was good at holding the ball up,' says Furlong.

The manager by this point was Glenn Roeder, who started with the pair in 12 of the first 17 matches. That was until Furlong was sent off in consecutive away matches against Millwall and Birmingham, which meant the partnership had a break before reuniting with potent consequences.

In nine matches at the turn of the year, they scored 14 goals between them, including both scoring twice in a 4-4 draw against Leicester City. The match prior to that, Dyer had also scored two against local rivals Luton.

'I'll never forget that Glenn had this brand new BMW 318is – a great looking motor,' says a man who knows his cars. 'He said to Bruce, "If you score twice you can have this motor for the weekend," and he did score twice!' Furlong laughs, revealing his glistening golden tooth. 'Whether he gave him the car, I'm not too sure, but that was the deal before the game.'

Dyer had accelerated onto the scene and, before we knew it, he sped off down the road to South London, sold to Crystal Palace for £1.25m in March. 'Bruce was the first to go and he kind of left me behind. I remember having a conversation with him and he was telling me that I could do it too,' says Furlong.

At that time Dyer was the most expensive teenager in Britain. On the day that he was sold to Premier League-bound Crystal Palace, another teenager had been coming back from football training in the rain when he heard the news on the radio. The windows in the car driven by his mother had been misted up with condensation due to the heat caused by his exertions and frustrations. The lack of a clear view left him claustrophobic and concerned. He read the paper, as he would always do, on the tube to school the next day and wondered how exciting it must be to be a Palace fan, being able to add Dyer to your armory just like that.

Perhaps Furlong wasn't the only one who had a seed of uncertainty planted in his mind by Dyer's departure. Footballers can move from club to club but being a fan is for life, isn't it?

The three games that followed Dyer's departure were as bad as his name made them sound. They lost 1-0 at Notts County, 3-0 at home to Grimsby Town and 2-0 at Sunderland. Three defeats on the spin left the club second from bottom – enough to test any teenager's loyalty.

Furlong only scored three goals in his last 12 matches but two loanees stepped into the void left by Dyer and helped keep the team in the division. Dennis Bailey scored four in five matches, including three in a row from the substitutes' bench. Tommy Mooney also arrived, like a whirlwind, and he added goals, including one against his parent club, Southend, as Watford won five of their last seven games to avoid relegation that had at one stage looked a certainty.

The final day of the season took the Hornets to Selhurst Park, home of Bruce Dyer and the newly-elected champions. Watford won 2-0 but the Eagles had already lifted off for the Premiership with Dyer in their talons.

The vultures were circling over Paul Furlong too. Any striker who scores 19 goals in a struggling team is going to be seen as easy pickings for one of the big teams.

'My mindset was that if you produce the goods for yourself, the rest will come,' says Furlong. 'When I was scoring those goals I wasn't doing it to impress A, B or C – I was doing it for myself. And if I did that, the rest would fall into place.'

And as things fell into place for Furlong, the boy's world fell apart. He didn't know it at the time, but Furlong was talking to other clubs behind his back.

'Glenn Roeder pulled me in and told me that they had interest from Chelsea and they wanted to speak to me,' says Furlong. 'I didn't have an agent at the time but my former manager at Enfield, Mike Ferguson, who had a wealth of footballing knowledge, came with me to Chelsea to give me some advice.'

Furlong didn't need much convincing – not when the man sitting opposite him at the table was former Tottenham and England international midfielder Glenn Hoddle. Chelsea were prepared to pay £2.3m – almost double the fee Crystal Palace had paid for Dyer, which had been a record for the Hornets.

It was time to move on.

So the boy who lived not far from where Furlong himself had grown up in Wood Green faced a predicament.

Could Furlong's departure force him to do the unthinkable? Was it too late to change allegiances? Could he stroll into the playground one day and declare himself a Chelsea fan? Would he be able to ride out the ridicule? Could he cope with the blow to his credibility? Surely it was something only the spineless could do. Surely no man is bigger than the club. He was a Watford fan, not a Paul Furlong fan.

His dilemma would eat away at his soul for the entire summer. The World Cup in the USA, which went ahead without England and was bookended by farcical penalties taken by Diana Ross and Roberto Baggio, did nothing to help him make a decision.

The wounds were still raw. When he saw a photo of Paul Furlong in his new Chelsea shirt it was like having salt rubbed into those wounds.

As the summer wore on, Watford moved on. They signed a replacement – Jamie Moralee, from Millwall. The most notable thing about him at the time was that he was going out with the EastEnders star Danniella Westbrook. He'd read about that in the new magazine of the moment, *Loaded*.

Few players would have been able to fill Furlong's boots in the youngster's eyes, and it was quite clear very early on that Moralee was definitely not that man. He may have had a certain prowess with the ladies, but not in front of goal.

Meanwhile, Furlong was readying himself for the step up, confident that playing for a big London club would not change him. 'My parents were honest, working-class people and had to work hard for what they had, so they are just qualities that were instilled growing up,' he says.

'You see your mother and father working and you see that they can't afford to give you what you want but there is always a meal on the table. It can be educational at times. I couldn't always have what I wanted and my friends would have things that my family couldn't necessarily afford, but I guess I've always been humble and really appreciated what I have.'

As the season began, Furlong's absence made the boy's heart grow fonder. He suspected Watford would lack punch without the big man and, as they failed to score in four of the first five games, his hunch was proved right. The only goal in those five matches came from Craig Ramage in an unconvincing League Cup win over Southend watched by just over 4,500 people, including the boy, at Vicarage Road.

Three days earlier Furlong had started his career with

Chelsea and had scored in a 2-0 win over Norwich. In fact, he hit the net in his new kit four times in the first seven games of the season. The transition had been seamless on the field but eye-opening off it.

'When you go to somewhere like Chelsea, there's much more media presence, a bigger fan base and there are celebrities in the players' lounge after the game,' says Furlong.

'When you're playing you're just living it, but now I look back and think, "Bloody hell I played with Ruud Gullit." I was rubbing shoulders with some superstars.'

It was the sight of Furlong playing and scoring for Chelsea that brought the turbulent times to a head for the boy. The departure of his favourite player had taken him to a crossroads. Chelsea were in the Premier League and scoring goals for fun. Watford were bumping along in the First Division. They were a fashionable London club – even if they had to wear a disturbing grey and orange kit away from home. Watford were always going to be Little Old Watford.

To amplify the dilemma he faced, it coincided with having to make his GCSE choices. In his mind he could not weigh up which decision would have the most far-reaching consequences for his life. In the end, he realised that he could apply the same criteria to both conundrums.

Was he willing to sacrifice history for geography? Would he opt for the creativity and flamboyance of art and drama or the practical functionality of design and technology? Did he want to speak the more popular French or unfashionable German? By a process of elimination, the boy made his decision.

Twenty years on, Furlong is into the next phase of his career as a coach at Queens Park Rangers – one of the nine clubs in the Football League he played for in 19 seasons as a professional. His background and upbringing had taught him the value of discipline and hard work, and that enabled him to play into his forties. Now he's a coach at QPR, where his two sons Darnell and Darian are trying to make it in the game.

The life of a professional player presents many difficult decisions but Furlong has one piece of advice: 'Whenever you're in a position to move from one club to another, try to make it an easy transition. I had a 22-year career that took me from non-league to the Premier League and back and now that I'm a coach I'm coming up against people I played with. If you don't burn your bridges, people will like you for it.'

And what about the teenage boy who almost swapped Watford for Chelsea in 1994? Twenty years on he rarely has call to use the history, design and technology or German qualifications he opted for at GCSE level. But he has never forgotten that summer when his loyalty was tested to the extent that he considered burning his bridges with the club he loved in order to follow a player he idolised. He's certain he made the right decision.

They say you should never meet your heroes but the boy is glad he got the chance to meet his.

# NICK WRIGHT

**On scoring <u>that</u> goal at Wembley**
'People come up to me and
say they named their children
Nick or Nicki so I do realise
what it means to people.'

# 6

Nick Wright played fewer than 50 first team matches in a Watford shirt and yet his contribution to the club's history is one of the most significant of all.

He arrived with Allan Smart in the summer of 1998. They were written off before they'd even played a match but at the end of the season they scored the two goals at Wembley to take Watford to the Premiership.

If you were there that day, you can probably close your eyes and re-live the moment when Nick Wright contorted his body and connected with the ball under the warm Wembley sunshine...

# NICK WRIGHT

ON May 31 for the rest of his life, Watford fans will contact Nick Wright to share their memories of one of the greatest days in the club's history. These days Twitter means that fans and players can connect in a way that has not always been possible.

> @foreignhornet
> 15 years since THAT goal from @NickWright! !
> Still remains one of the best days of my life!

> @Wivster1
> Nicky Wright Wright Wright. #whataday

> @mjones1881
> Tap in!

> @geetachurchy
> I wrote a song about your goal :)

> @mjapeter
> Best goal ever scored at Wembley. Irrefutable.

There were many messages like that on the 15th anniversary of Watford's first and (so far) only victory at Wembley. And there will be many more when May 31 comes around again, particularly when the day dawns bright and sunny as it did in 1999, and the memories of making that trip to north-west London come flooding back.

A football club's history is made up of moments and there are very few finer ones than Nick Wright's goal at Wembley. Watford had played at Wembley before but they had not won there, nor had they scored, so Wright's goal in the 38th minute of the play-off final against Bolton Wanderers was the first.

It is not our natural bias talking when we say that Nick Wright's goal was one of the finest the old Wembley Stadium ever witnessed. His spectacular overhead kick was a stunning moment of instinctive invention that would have graced any game beneath the Twin Towers.

When you look back at moments that define a player's career, that is undoubtedly it for Nick Wright. That goal, the first in a 2-0 victory that took Watford to the Premiership, was one of the most significant single contributions to the club's history. The fact that Wright made only a handful of further appearances for Watford before injury ended his career adds extra poignancy to that moment.

So for Watford supporters, May 31 shall forever be known as St Nicholas's Day. The Patron Saint of Overhead Kicks.

'It's really nice to read those messages,' he says when we meet. 'A few of my mates at home have a bit of a laugh saying, "You can stop milking it now." But it's nice that it's the first thing that comes to mind on that day. When people describe it as the best day of their lives, wow, yeah, it hits home just what an impact we had on a number of Watford people's lives.'

\* \* \*

Like Craig Ramage, Nick Wright is a Derbyshire lad. He came through the Rams youth team and remembers many of the same people – Arthur Cox and Roy McFarland. He remembers beating Manchester United's Class of 1992 when he was part of the Derby County youth team.

His biggest regret, he says, is not making his first-team debut for Derby. 'I got very close, I got on the bench, but I didn't get on,' he says. 'We were a very good youth team but Derby had spent a lot of money on players so it was hard for the young players to make the jump from the reserve team to the first team. I was ambitious and I wanted to get on, so I knocked on the manager's door and asked to go on loan. Jim Smith was the gaffer and when I did that he said, "Okay, you can go to Carlisle." I still believe he said that to put me off because Jim did say they wanted me for the first team but I knew I had to play.

'I didn't know where Carlisle was. I knew it was north but I had no idea how far north. It was November. It was miserable and cold. I went up on the Thursday but training was cancelled on the Friday because of a waterlogged pitch so I made my debut for Carlisle on the Saturday without having even trained with them.

'I was lucky because Carlisle, and a lot of clubs like Carlisle, watch a lot of reserve team football so they'd seen me play behind the front two at Derby, and they afforded me the luxury of doing that sometimes. That's how I struck up a bond with Allan Smart. As a front player he was brilliant at holding the ball up and bringing players into the game. His first touch was as good as anyone's for a six-foot-plus player. He's got fantastic feet. What this meant was that Smarty liked playing with his back to goal and I had the energy to run in and beyond. It meant our games matched up brilliantly well. I'd do the running, moving players around, which gave Allan lots of space with the ball.'

It was one of those nervy Tuesday nights towards the end

of the season. The pace of Watford's promotion challenge had slowed. A defeat at Gillingham was followed by three consecutive 1-1 draws. A last-gasp win at home to Bristol Rovers, when Tommy Mooney charged up from the back, bulldozing his way through the opposition defence to score a late winner, had just about kept Watford on the rails but then came a home defeat to Walsall and another couple of draws. One win in eight was certainly not promotion-winning form.

And so when Carlisle United arrived after their long journey from the north-west, bringing a tiny group of fans with them, they had nothing to lose. They were deep in trouble and ended up going down but Wright and Smart caused the Watford defence no end of problems that night.

'We were a very young team and we were learning as we were playing,' says Wright. 'There was so much talent in that team, we shouldn't have got relegated, but we were naïve. Our defensive play – and I don't mean just from our defenders – was too open. We attacked at every opportunity but we'd also concede a lot. We beat Kevin Keegan's Fulham that season, but lost to them 5-0 in the away game, so that showed the two sides to the Carlisle team.

'So against Watford we weren't thinking about keeping it respectable – we were trying to win the game and we were the better team by a long way. Within half an hour, Watford made a tactical change and they had Steve Palmer man-mark me. I'd never experienced that before and it was strange. We'd come to play a team that was going to get promoted to Division One and they were man-marking me. Steve was tough to play against. He stuck to his task and I think he'd admit that he was quite happy not to be involved in the game if it meant he kept me out of the game. It was very, very difficult to try to make runs when somebody was following me everywhere.'

Somehow, Watford prevailed, winning 2-1, and after the

Carlisle players trooped off the pitch, they found someone waiting for them outside their dressing room.

'At the end of the game, the manager [Graham Taylor] stood at the entrance to the away dressing room and shook our hands as we went in. I'd never experienced that before – or since. There we were, being congratulated for our performance by a former England manager, even though we'd lost 2-1.'

Wright had initially joined Carlisle on a month's loan but agreed to sign for Carlisle until the end of the season. He had a clause in his Carlisle contract that said he could leave if anyone offered £100,000.

'At the end of the season I went to speak to Chesterfield, which would have been the easy option because it was on my doorstep, but I wasn't inspired by their chairman or his knowledge of football, so that didn't appeal to me,' he says. 'I spoke to Dario Gradi at Crewe and that was the opposite. That did appeal because of the style of play and the way they developed talent.

'But I came down to Watford and was immediately impressed by Graham Taylor. It was really important to him that I'd fit in as a person as well as a player. There was absolutely no guarantee of playing but the one question I asked him was, "If I prove I'm good enough will I be playing in your first-team this season?" He said that if I proved myself, I would.'

The perception was that Nick Wright and Allan Smart were a package deal but Wright did not know his team-mate would be following him down to Vicarage Road. It was only when Wright said he was joining Watford that Smart revealed he too had agreed to sign.

Wright cost Watford £100,000, Smart cost an initial £75,000 (which would double after 40 games). Meanwhile, Bristol City – the side that had followed Watford up out of the Second Division – splashed £2.2m on forwards Ade Akinbiyi and

Tony Thorpe. That June, a disgruntled fan wrote to the *Watford Observer* complaining about a perceived lack of ambition: 'The second reason [for increasing season ticket prices] was for the funding of new players and GT promised that Premiership players would be top of the list. So who the hell are Allan Smart and Nick Wright? Bristol City have spent £2.2m, which proves their intentions for the new season. We spend £175,000 on two Carlisle rejects.'

'I don't mind someone saying that,' says Wright, 'but unless they can stand back and say, "I was wrong," they shouldn't say it. He might have been right if we had bombed, but we turned out to be pretty good value for money.

'As a fan you are absolutely entitled to an opinion – you're investing money to go and watch the team – but it shows a lack of confidence in the manager's knowledge and experience in football to say that before you've seen us play. Anyone who thinks that signing someone for a million means you're guaranteeing a good player, well, over the last 20 years or so you can see it doesn't. Some of the players Watford have signed for big money have totally bombed. It's a case of getting the right player, the right person, who will contribute to making a winning team. It doesn't have to be a big signing, it has to be the right fit.'

But did Wright read the letter in the newspaper? Did it fire him up?

'I read it. Anyone who says footballers don't read is talking garbage. I like to read. I liked to see what people were saying about me and about the team. But it didn't motivate me or upset me because I didn't need anything to motivate me. I wanted to play my best and see what level I could get to in my career. But I remembered it, and other people remembered it, my family remembered it. I remember talking to my dad about it. He's very level-headed, my dad, and maybe it was something he hoped I would prove wrong. I think that to make a snap judgement before I'd even played a game was ill-advised.'

Smart was involved with the first-team right from the start of the 1998-99 season. He started the opening league game at Portsmouth and scored his first goal in a 4-1 defeat at Sunderland not long afterwards. Wright had to wait a little longer.

'I'd played during pre-season and I felt I'd done quite well. I'd played in the reserves and scored and the first-team had had a bit of an indifferent start. They'd lost a couple in a row and although I'd travelled with the squad, I'd not been involved,' he says.

Remembering the pledge that Graham Taylor had made him when he signed, Wright went to knock on the manager's office door.

'I didn't ask any of the senior players whether they thought it was a good idea to do this – I suspect they probably would have told me not to – but I don't like things festering. I'd rather go and have a conversation and find out exactly where I stood. I told Graham I was disappointed not to have played. I said I felt I'd been training well and I took him back to the conversation we'd had when I signed. I said the reason I'd joined was that I'd get a chance. He didn't say much. He listened, and he didn't give me any indication there was a problem with me going in to speak to him but that was that. He didn't make me any promises and so I left the room.

'The next game was away at Huddersfield and he picked me to make my first team debut in the luxury position in the hole behind the two strikers. I like to think it was a positive thing going to see him and that it convinced the manager to give me an opportunity.

'The game didn't go so well,' he adds. 'We lost 2-0 and we got battered, really. I had an absolute shocker. I didn't get into the game at all and if the manager had never picked me again

I could not have complained. He'd given me the opportunity and I didn't take it – didn't take it at all. He didn't say anything but I didn't need the manager to tell me I'd not played well. I hadn't contributed anything. I hadn't done my job. I was not happy with my performance and I was worried that might be it for a while.

'The next game was at home to QPR – a local derby, a big game for the fans. They had Vinny Jones and some other big names. Graham could easily have left me out but he stuck with me. Fortunately, I don't think too many Watford fans had gone up to Huddersfield on the Tuesday night so not many people had seen how bad I'd been.

'This was a totally new experience. I got into the game early, I had the beating of my marker and I went past him, had a few shots and created chances. I got the man of the match award afterwards and from then on I was involved until the end of the season.'

And what a season it turned out to be.

* * *

Wright played in a variety of roles for Graham Taylor and learned all about forward play in the process. He played up front, partnering Gifton Noel-Williams at times. Sometimes he tucked in behind the two strikers and towards the end of the season he spent more time on the right-hand side, sometimes playing deeper as a conventional wide midfielder, often pushing up to make a three-man strike force. The variety of styles and the flexibility to move around depending on the way a game was going suited Wright, who could run and run until he dropped.

'I was a fit player but we were a fit team,' he says. 'When I was at Derby as a youngster I would always win the long-distance run. When I first got to Watford and did the cross-country round Cassiobury Park, I was fifth or sixth.

'Graham wanted me to play a very high intensity game. He didn't want me to pace myself and hold myself back to last 90 minutes. He said if he had to take me off after 70 or 75 minutes that was what he had subs for. He wanted me to be all-action, sprinting to close defenders down and make space rather than just running. He encouraged me to play that high-tempo game until I had nothing left.

'It was part of his plan to be able to get forward quickly, break quickly and take the game from one end of the pitch to the other. He told us all the stats – that a really high percentage of goals are scored in an imaginary arc that goes from the corner of the six-yard box to just outside the 18-yard box. That's where goals come from and so unless the ball is in that area you're not gonna score.

'Now that made playing very simple and very enjoyable because we all knew what the objective was and what our jobs were. Get the ball into those dangerous positions and make sure we had men in there to meet it.

'Earlier in my career, wingers stayed predominantly near the touchline but that wasn't how we played. If I was on the right and the ball was on the left-hand side, I moved over to become a second striker. My job was to go in at the far post and I knew that if I wasn't there I'd not done my job and Graham would remind me. There were goals to be had there – tap-ins. At home to Crewe I scored from about two yards because I was there at the far post. I wouldn't have scored that if I hadn't been learning from Graham Taylor because I timed my run in front of the defender as the ball came across from Peter Kennedy.'

One of Wright's best games in a Watford shirt came at the end of January 1999, against top-of-the-table Sunderland. Tony Daley caused havoc on the wing and Wright partnered Noel-Williams up front, scoring the first with a header after he slipped his marker. Noel-Williams got the winner, after Niall Quinn had equalised, but then had to go off when he was on the receiving end of a very poor challenge, which ended his season.

For Wright, the victory over Sunderland proved what the team could do, although in the weeks that followed they struggled. A 2-1 win at Loftus Road – where Wright scored 'a dipping volley into the far corner, as I like to describe it' – was their only win in eight.

It was around this time that Graham Taylor brought in a psychologist called Ciaran Cosgrave, better known as Mr Pink Shirt.

'There was a bit of natural scepticism when he first came in,' says Wright. 'People wondered who he was and what he was going to do. Initially, he came in and just spent time with us and talked to us individually. He asked me about my short-term and long-term goals. Now, after ten or 11 years in the business world, asking myself that question is second nature because you'd have short, medium and long-term goals but in football, especially when I was young, I don't think I looked further than the next couple of months. He made me think about what I wanted to do, how I was going to achieve it and what barriers I would have to overcome.

'He also talked to us about our emotions and feelings. He was very strong on visualisation, which was not something I'd experienced before. He made us think about what would happen not just longer term but also in individual games. I started visualising the good things I wanted to do in games.

'The positive thing that happened was that it got all of us, the players, to spend a lot of time together as a group. We weren't rushing off after training, going our separate ways. We were becoming closer as a squad. We were working extremely hard physically and now we were working on our minds a bit more. You can't put it down to just having a psychologist but if it gave us an extra one per cent then it was worth doing. As we came together, we got into the habit of winning and we went into matches expecting to win. Three becomes four, becomes five and suddenly we were very, very hard to beat and the play-offs were back on.'

As those play-off matches approached, the belief in the squad increased. Although Wright felt he was already a positive person, he felt the energy around the place change. Suddenly everyone was moving in the same direction.

'It's interesting because in my work now I say, "What's the worst thing that can happen?" I find that the fear of failure stops people from doing things. I am fortunate that I've never had that. I will try my best to achieve whatever it is I'm trying to achieve and I won't worry about what it'll feel like to fail. You can learn from failure. You evaluate, you see what you can do better next time.

'I can't speak for the other players because I don't know if they had a fear of failure but what I do know is that we started talking to each other more. Our team meetings weren't just about tactics; we were discussing our feelings, our expectations of ourselves and others.

'During one session, Ciaran asked us to think about our favourite particular player and list three characteristics of that player and why they were our favourite.

'This is slightly controversial because although I played for Derby and I'm a Derby fan these days, when I grew up I was a Nottingham Forest fan. Half my family is Forest, the other half is Derby, so before I joined Derby I watched Forest a lot more. I grew up watching Stuart Pearce, Nigel Clough, and a young Roy Keane.

'So I said my favourite player was Stuart Pearce. I can't remember the three words I chose to sum him up, but one was patriotic and the others were probably committed and passionate, something like that. Anyway, Ciaran went round the group and wrote the words up on a flipchart.

'What we found was that only ten per cent of the words had anything to do with skill. The great majority of the words were behaviour or character traits. These were emotional reasons for liking or admiring a player, and they were very personal to each individual, but their technical or tactical ability, their skill as a footballer, did not feature as much as their attitudes.

'I think he was trying to get across to us that the higher you go in football, the more it becomes about those other factors. Commitment and desire can be the difference. Being scared of failure can lead to failure.'

\* \* \*

For the fans, the two play-off games against Birmingham City added up to 210 minutes of agony – 220 minutes if you include the penalty shoot-out at St Andrew's.

The home leg was tense. 'I remember lobbing the keeper and the ball skimmed the bar,' Wright says.

'We played with a front three – Michel Ngonge, Tommy Mooney and me – because we knew one of their centre halves was not so good on the ball. The idea was to isolate that player, press high up the pitch, pressurise Grainger and Rowett, who were decent on the ball, but let Michael Johnson have it and let him play the passes out of defence. Johnson was a good defender but he's not that great on the ball. It worked well for us because we won a lot of the ball quite high up the pitch.

'We had three or four great chances and we dominated a lot of the game but at the end all we had was Michel's header. At the end there was a bit of disappointment that we hadn't scored more to take a stronger hold on the tie.'

There was a fierce atmosphere at the away leg. 'We knew what it would be like because they could be a hostile crowd but in the warm-up, as we ran from side-to-side across the pitch, we were getting a lot of abuse from their fans on both sides of the ground.'

Watford had a nightmare start, conceding to a scrambled Dele Adebola goal after 90 seconds. 'The noise in the stadium after that goal was incredible and we were really up against it,' says Wright. 'But we still believed in our ability. Birmingham played very well and Alec Chamberlain made a number of excellent saves for us.'

David Holdsworth was sent off for Birmingham early in the second half, which eased the pressure a bit – not much, but a bit. Then came extra-time, by which time Wright had been substituted, his legs buckling after 87 minutes of chasing, closing down and running to stretch the Blues defence. Having been substituted in each of the previous seven games, as per Graham Taylor's plan, Wright had to sit and watch extra-time and then the agonising penalty shoot-out.

'We had practised penalties in training, going through the whole routine,' he says. 'We stood in the centre circle and walked up, placed the ball and took the penalty. I quite fancied taking one but I knew I probably wouldn't be on the pitch at the end.'

There's a photo of Wright, which appears in the book *Four Seasons*, taken during that penalty shoot-out. His hands are pressed together in prayer, his eyes are shut and he's hoping for the best knowing he can do no more to influence the result.

* * *

After a good celebration, Watford began to look forward to Wembley and the final against Bolton Wanderers. There was even more intensity to the training sessions. Little did anyone know at the time, but Wright could have missed the game after picking up an injury.

'I remember it vividly,' he says. 'It was not long after the Birmingham game and we finished the session with a small-sided game, which was common. I'd just gone past a player and was just about to shoot when I was clipped from behind by Micah so I took an air-shot.

'I felt a click in my pelvis and something didn't feel quite right. I didn't say anything to anyone but after I got home I iced it. The next day I tested it by running and there was still a niggle. It wasn't much more than that but it was certainly a little pain that I was aware of.

'I got through training on anti-inflammatories, which are common among players, and painkillers. I didn't tell anyone at the club I was struggling because I didn't want anyone to know I was carrying a problem.

'There was no way I was going to miss Wembley but there was also no way I would have taken someone else's place in the team if I knew I could not contribute in the way that was required. With anti-inflammatories and painkillers I could play. I kept testing myself and I could still sprint to my maximum and I could change direction. I could take the pain away and I could get through the game, although I don't think you'd recommend it to children.'

There was no sign of any ill-effects during the game. Wright was his usual energetic self and when Watford won a corner as half-time approached, he took up his position on the far corner of the 18-yard box.

'That was my position because the theory was the ball might get cleared by a defender and I'd be waiting,' he says. 'It was a great delivery from Peter Kennedy, very difficult for the goal-keeper and defenders, and Andy Todd managed to head it but could only head it up in the air. He didn't get a great deal of distance on it.'

As the ball fell to him, Wright did not have time to think about what he was going to do; instinct took over. However, he is clear on one thing... He intended to take a shot.

'I was not just helping the ball back into the box,' he says firmly. 'I knew I had two options from there: either lay it back or try what I did. There was no one to lay it back to so I was trying to hit it hard towards the goal. I wasn't just helping it back into the box, I was having an attempt at goal. Okay, I am not saying I was good enough to pick my spot, just above the defender's head, right in the top corner, but I was trying to execute a good technique and hit it cleanly with enough force to get it on target.

'It was an instinctive thing, all about technique and timing. It's not a natural thing to do so the only way to get my foot that high was to concentrate on getting off the ground. I knew I'd hit it well. When I landed on the floor I was looking between all the legs to see what had happened to the ball. I didn't see it clearly go in but I heard a shout of, "It's in!" and saw the net ripple a bit.

'Then I got up and ran towards where my parents were sitting in the crowd. I didn't make it very far because I got rugby-tackled by Paul Robinson – a typical Robbo challenge, really!'

Wright was replaced in the 87th minute by Alon Hazon. Allan Smart had been brought on a bit earlier. Wright had only just taken his seat on the bench when Smart made a crunching tackle in the centre circle and the ball broke to Hyde who played a neat pass to Peter Kennedy who, in turn, played the perfectly-weighted ball across to Smart, who had picked himself up and had charged up to the edge of the penalty area.

'It wasn't the conventional finish to go with the outside of the boot,' says Wright of his team-mate Smart's swerving shot that evaded the Bolton goalkeeper and flew into the net. 'When he scored, I sprinted down the touchline to celebrate with him.

'The celebrations after that were great. Most players don't get to experience that. People work in the game for 40 years and don't come close so I count myself very lucky. It was an awesome experience. Whether it sunk in at the time, possibly not, but now, looking back, I realise we changed the lives of the supporters. We created something that people remember years later and that is still so special.

'At the time it really wasn't about me – genuinely. It wasn't about me scoring a goal, it was about the team winning. If we'd won 1-0 with the ball stumbling in off the back of someone's thigh, that would have felt the same.

'If I'd scored that goal and we'd lost 2-1, people would not be looking back so fondly. But having said that, these days I am pleased. I am glad that Michel Ngonge didn't get a touch on it.'

The two rejects from Carlisle United did okay, didn't they?

And what about Bristol City and their £2.2m strikers? They finished 24th, bottom of the table, and were relegated.

* * *

Once the celebrations were over and the fact that he was now a Premiership player had sunk in, Nick Wright became concerned that the pain in his groin was not easing. 'I went on holiday and it hadn't got any better,' he says.

'I was swimming and it didn't feel right so I went to have an x-ray. That x-ray showed that a piece of bone in my pelvis was fractured. It was an avulsion fracture, where the tendon had pulled a piece of the bone away. If we'd known that earlier, I wouldn't have played at Wembley.

'We let it heal but the muscles in my groin had weakened. I played a few games – I started the match at West Ham and was sub against Chelsea and at Arsenal and Manchester United but it became clear I needed a hernia operation.

'It was so disappointing not to do myself justice in the Premier League so I knew I had to have the operation and get myself sorted.'

The operation was a success and after playing well in a couple of reserve games, he was picked for the FA Cup tie at home to Birmingham City.

'I had a decent game but I started to flag after about 65 minutes,' he says. 'Graham took me off near the end. We were losing 1-0 and I'd been playing quite well and so the crowd booed when I was substituted. Watford fans don't boo Graham Taylor, as you know, so I don't think he was particularly happy with that. He was fine with me because I'd done well but maybe the fans didn't realise I was tiring.

'He then asked me to play in a reserve game against Coventry on the Tuesday night. In hindsight perhaps I didn't need to play in that game because I'd played more than an hour for the first team and I was training well.

'Seven minutes into the game I collided with their goalkeeper – 15 stone Steve Ogrizovic. I'd run past the full-back, then tried to slip the ball past Ogrizovic but it hit his knee, then bounced back to me and so we collided at full pelt. It was a similar collision to the one that had ended Brian Clough's career.'

Wright tried to play on but after ten minutes or so, he turned and his leg crumpled under him. A scan did not show any serious damage so after a couple of weeks of rest, he returned to the training ground to start running.

'One of the key parts of my game was speed but also stamina,' he says. 'I could sustain a fast pace for a long period of time. A lot of players can sprint for ten yards but I had the capacity to sprint for 50 yards, take a short break and then do another 50 yards.

'We were doing this running exercise with the physio and I was struggling. I was lagging behind and the physio put it down to a lack of effort. That sort of still grinds with me because one thing I was never accused of was a lack of effort. I might have had a shocker at times, the ball might bounce off me, but it was not for a lack of effort.

'I walked off the training pitch really disgruntled about that and I demanded another scan. This time it showed serious damage to the cartilage in my knee.'

That started a painful three-year battle to regain his fitness – a fight that was ultimately unsuccessful. By the time he retired, Graham Taylor had left, so too had Gianluca Vialli, and Ray Lewington had become the manager. All that time, Wright was engaged in a private, and sometimes very lonely, struggle to recover from the injury.

There were glimmers of hope that he might get back to full strength but they were fleeting moments. Instead of flying down the wing, he spent his time lying on the operating table and in the treatment room.

'Initially, the idea was to have an operation to trim the cartilage,' he says. 'My understanding was that I would be out for three or four weeks and things seemed to be going to plan. I played a game at wing back for the reserves at West Ham and I was getting up and down the line well. I began to think I might be close to getting back into the first team. After the game my knee began to swell. Sometimes that happens with injuries but it kept happening. Apart from the swelling, the knee felt great. I felt strong and my movement was great. It was decided I would need a second knee operation. After that operation it never felt the same again.

'In hindsight I wish I'd given it longer. I wish I'd never had that operation. I should have given the muscles around the knee longer to rebuild their strength. But there are a lot of pressures. I was a young player and I certainly didn't have the patience. I wanted to be playing, the club wanted me to be playing. I was keen to get back as quickly as possible.

'In the months after my operation, a number of players went to see a surgeon in Denver, Colorado, to see Richard Steadman, who is one of the leading people in the world. I wish I'd explored something like that.

'Unfortunately, the knee was never the same. I got back to about 90 per cent but I could never bend it fully. The mobility wasn't the same. It may not sound like a lot of difference between 90 and 100 per cent but that is the difference between being a professional footballer and not being a professional footballer. In the end, I had a third operation and I spent three years working to get back.

'It was the toughest time I have experienced but the well-wishes from the fans were great. I was probably in as good physical condition as any of the other players but in the back of my mind I knew my knee was not making any progress.

'It was a demoralising time. You lose your relationships with the players, you don't feel part of the team, you're not contributing. For anyone who is not mentally strong, I could see how it could affect them for the rest of their lives. I built up a very good friendship with one of the physios, Luke Anthony, and I think he understood what I was going through.

'Ray Wilkins was very encouraging when he was the coach and I trained with the first team a few times but I just couldn't get there. Ray Lewington was very accommodating too. When it finally came to make the decision, it wasn't really that hard, but I am very grateful to Watford for allowing me the time to try to recover. They could have terminated my contract and paid up – although I'm not sure how well that would have gone down publicly – but they didn't. They gave me every chance.'

Wright's final appearance for the Watford first-team was on September 26, 2000, in a League Cup defeat against Notts County. He finally retired in March 2003. In the meantime, he'd had trials at Sheffield United and Bristol Rovers. 'I played a reserve game for Sheffield United and although I scored and set one up, Neil Warnock said that although I was contributing he could see my mobility was not there.'

\* \* \*

Wright was 27 when he made the transition from footballer to ex-footballer. He could see the end coming and had time to adjust but it was still a shock. 'I'd done well at school up to the age of 16 but I hadn't done A-Levels or a degree, which I would have done if I had not chosen football, so I was in a really difficult situation,' he says. 'People imagine you're set for life but it isn't anything like that. Watford offered me a coaching role with the under-15s but we didn't get as far as discussing money because I'd still have needed a full-time job. I think Watford felt obliged to offer me something but I didn't want to be a charity case. I had a young family and I knew that if I got a full-time job and did some coaching I wouldn't see them so I had to find a job.'

By coincidence, he started working for the mobile phone retailer Phones4U – a company that had sponsored Watford's shirts during their season in the Premier League. 'There was no link with the club at all – I just found myself in an assessment centre at Phones4U applying for a job I had no real intention of getting. It wasn't what I really wanted to do but they offered me a store manager role. I still didn't really want it but I thought I'd give it a try. My manager said to me, "Run the store as though you're running a successful football team." I spent

11 years with them, starting in the store and then progressing through to training all the new starters.'

In September 2014, Phones4U closed and Wright tweeted: '11 years in football, loved it, wore the number 11 shirt. 11 years at Phones4U, loved it. What will the next 11 years hold?'

Although Wright has no regrets, he does admit that 'not a day goes by when I don't think about football'.

He adds: 'I'm 38 now and I like to think that I'd just be coming to the end of my career now. I think I would have kept myself very fit but the reality is, my career ended 15 years ago, really.'

His young sons are currently Manchester City and Chelsea supporters, although he takes them to watch Derby County and Watford and he hopes that, slowly, they are being persuaded of the merits of watching them. His partner, Steph, is a Forest fan and he admits it's probably too late for her to see the light now.

Like Craig Ramage, Wright has suffered the disappointment of seeing 'his' team lose in consecutive play-off finals at Wembley but he said that going to Watford's game against Crystal Palace in May 2013 stirred the emotions.

'I enjoyed being on Wembley Way, among the fans, because that was the one thing you miss out on as a player,' he says. 'Graham Taylor tried to shield us from that a little bit because he didn't want the adrenaline to build up, he didn't want us full of nervous energy. But to witness the build-up, to be in that atmosphere, is incredible. There's not a lot of singing – it's a very nervous, edge-of-the-seat occasion.

'I know we didn't go to Wembley in 1999 to enjoy the day, not at all. We went to win the game. Nothing else matters other than the result. Look at Derby against QPR. Derby hammered them but QPR scored in the last minute and Harry Redknapp is the hero.'

Although Wright played fewer than 50 games for Watford and was a regular for just one season, his name is etched into the club's history, like one of the main characters in a fairytale.

His Wembley goal, and Allan Smart's that followed it, sparked some of the wildest celebrations Watford supporters have ever enjoyed. Until Troy Deeney's goal against Leicester City in the 2013 play-off semi-final, many might have put Wright's down as the greatest Watford goal they'd ever seen.

Wright was at Vicarage Road, working as a radio commentator, and so he witnessed the incredible rollercoaster of emotions at the end of that Leicester match. 'The circumstances were incredible,' he says.

'Knockaert dived, so already there was a bit of anger, and I certainly articulated that on the radio. He bought the penalty, so for Manuel Almunia to save it, then the double save, was amazing. Within 15 seconds the ball went down the right wing, went across the box and Deeney fires it in to take Watford to Wembley. It was an amazing moment and there was a video clip of me, Derek Payne, Craig Ramage and Jon Marks [the BBC Three Counties commentary team] screaming. They showed it on SoccerAM. That's what football can do to you.'

Deeney's goal was a remarkable team goal and a decisive, almost defiant finish. The extreme turnaround in fortunes, from despair to joy in under a minute, caused palpitations, but for some the sight of Nicky Wright's shot sailing over the Bolton goalkeeper and defenders into the roof of the Wembley net will never be beaten.

Perhaps if Watford had done the business against Crystal Palace in the Wembley final, Deeney's goal would have the same enduring significance.

The difference with Wright's goal was that the end result was the one we all wanted. As brilliant as the overhead kick was, you get the feeling that Wright would have been just as happy with a tap-in from two yards at the back post. Maybe.

As we're preparing to go our separate ways, Wright reveals that whenever he enters a Fantasy Football game he names his team 'From Hero to Zero'. 'That sums up my Watford career because it went a bit like that,' he says.

I have to correct him there. Nick Wright will always be a Watford hero. He'll always be remembered on May 31 – as will the rest of the victorious Watford team.

Perhaps you'll pull out this book and re-read this chapter next time the anniversary comes around.

If that's the case, have a happy St Nicholas's Day.

# RAY LEWINGTON

**On getting the Watford job**
'Oli Phillips rang to tell me I'd
got one per cent of the vote in a
poll in the Watford Observer
asking who the next manager
should be. I told him that was
probably my mum voting.'

## 7

Ray Lewington was under no illusions when he took the Watford job. He knew the brief was to cut costs to the bone and avoid relegation. Simple.

Maybe it wasn't pretty at times but Lewington guided the club to the semi-final of the FA Cup and the Carling Cup – and the threat of dropping down a division was kept at bay.

When Lewington had steered the club through the choppy waters, just as he could see a glimmer of hope on the horizon, Watford sacked him.

There's not a trace of bitterness, though. Here he reflects on the most turbulent time in the club's history and offers some revelations too.

# RAY LEWINGTON

It's fitting that we meet somewhere resembling a space station. Above us is a huge circular ceiling, deep purple in colour, which is punctuated by crisp crystal spotlights that look like stars shining from a distant galaxy. The structure of the building around us is white, elegant, bold and curved at every opportunity.

The floor far beneath is a lunar lake of pristine marble. It's being guarded by lamps with tripod legs, which appear to wear flamboyant headdresses of sculpted metal animated by iridescent light.

This is the future. Of English football, at least. This is St George's Park.

We are in a completely different world to the last time I interviewed Ray Lewington.

Then, nine years earlier, against a backdrop of a marigold-coloured wall in a room barely illuminated by the sort of strip lights you'd see on the ceiling of a school corridor, we wandered through Watford's canteen as the players sat around the wooden-topped tables next to the serving hatch.

We headed into an adjacent meeting room where there was an overhead projector and a pile of cloth-covered chairs, thread-bare in places, stacked unevenly next to the wall, the whole place almost self-conscious of its bubbling, peeling paintwork.

People often say to Lewington now, 'You've done all right since then.' And they're right. He's now the England assistant manager, and we're sitting in the luxurious lobby of the hotel that is built on the site of the St George's Park complex in Burton where England prepare for international matches.

Back then, in January 2005, Lewington was preparing for the second leg of the League Cup semi-final against Liverpool. It turned out to be the final high point at his time at Watford. Just over three months later, he was sacked – for the only time in his long career.

We take a seat in the vast reception area and sip from fine-lipped coffee cups as we talk. In a few days, England will fly to America for some preparation games before heading on to Brazil for the World Cup. Gary Cahill wanders past, deep in conversation on his mobile. Later, Roy Hodgson enquires politely, as you would expect, how long Lewington will be. 'Not long, not long,' he says in his South London accent.

Through the large windows, we can spot the famous, and not so famous, faces of players past and present who probably see St George's Park as some kind of footballing university. They head from the patchwork quilt of immaculate football pitches, across the smart carpeted paths to the restaurants before heading back out to the training ground, or perhaps the classroom, to continue their education. This is where a generation of coaches are being prepared for the uncertain world of football management as they make their way through their UEFA qualifications.

It is perhaps symbolic that as this new wave of coaches mill around beneath us they may catch sight of Lewington sitting above. He may not be the most flamboyant or glamorous of characters, he has never been one for a soundbite and he has certainly never courted publicity or controversy, but Lewington serves as a fine example to any aspiring football coach.

'I have done all right,' he says humbly, almost reluctantly, before revealing his inner confidence and resilience. 'I think it probably proves I was right not to let anything affect me.'

Then comes a warning to those who think it is easy to stay in the game as long as he has – nearly three decades of almost continuous service as a coach or manager. 'Get your head down and move on. Because you never know what's around the corner, that's for sure. Don't try to predict what happens in football. You've got no chance.'

Here we look back, through his eyes, at his turbulent journey to this point, focusing on his time at Watford, which featured highs, lows, several days when he was at the centre of some dramatic breaking news, as well as a couple of heart-breaking moments.

## APRIL 2001
## ............WE'RE JUST HEARING RAY LEWINGTON HAS RESIGNED AS MANAGER OF BRENTFORD...........

I'd had a row with my chairman, Ron Noades, which is very easy to do. We got on well but Ron had been manager of the team for a while and had his ideas about the club and what he wanted to do. He wanted me to resign and I wouldn't do it. Ron was one of those people that you could never get the better of. I knew he'd make it very difficult for me. I could see him selling all the players, leaving me high and dry. I called my best mate, Ray Wilkins – he's been my best mate since we were ten years old – and I told him the situation. I said: 'I've just got to get out of there. Really, I have got to get out of there.'

He said: 'Listen, you've got to keep it really secret but Vialli's going to Watford, and, if he does, I'm going to be his number two, and there's a place for a reserve team manager.' I told him: 'I'll have it. That'll do me. I'll go and resign from Brentford and I'll be there!'

..........THIS JUST IN: RAY LEWINGTON HAS BEEN
APPOINTED AS RESERVE TEAM MANAGER AT
WATFORD, AND WILL JOIN GIANLUCA VIALLI'S
BACKROOM STAFF..........

I really enjoyed getting out on the pitch again as a coach.
Basically I was with all the youngsters who were coming
through. Luca had a big squad of first-team players that he
picked from, like they have abroad, and he didn't really take
too much interest in what I was doing, which was fine.

I had a nice little young squad with some half-decent
players in, like Ashley Young. It was great being away from
Brentford and all the stuff that Ron was throwing at me.

Our matches were mostly midweek, so after doing a
morning session with the reserves on a Saturday, Luca was
sending me out scouting. I'd go to watch a player or do
a report on the opposition. It was good to step back and
see it from a different angle. When you're the manager,
your head is down and you're watching your own team and
everything just flashes by.

But when you go to watch a match where you're not
actually concerned about the result or how your own team
is playing, you just watch it for what it is and sometimes
you learn a lot more when you're not under that pressure.

Sometimes, as a manager, you think you know what
you've seen, but the pressure distorts it. Sometimes I'd
think a player had done quite well and then I'd watch the
video and see he'd been bloody awful. But at the time it was
all right, usually because the result has masked it. You've
probably sneaked a one-nil and everyone's happy.

Luca came in and introduced the European way, which
every club has embraced now, all these years on. At the
time it was new for many clubs, particularly at our level,

to get into sports science, diet, nutrition, measuring body
fat. They're commonplace now but they weren't then. Luca
came in and got everything changed in the canteen. He got
all the right foods put in there and educated the players on
how to live and how to become a footballer, which I think
we needed. English clubs needed that.

Watford, certainly, were a traditional old English club,
which lived on the old values – things that they'd been
doing year-in, year-out, and suddenly Luca came in and
said, right, all of that, out the window.

He said this was the way we were going to do things
from now on and he completely changed the mindset.
Although he didn't particularly get too much success on the
field, off the field he laid the foundations for what every
other manager has built on. Things that are accepted as the
norm, he started, and so he left a legacy of some sort.

## FEBRUARY 2002
..... THERE'S ACTION ON THE WAY FROM ST ANDREWS,
WHERE BIRMINGHAM CITY CONDEMNED WATFORD
TO THEIR SIXTH DEFEAT IN TEN MATCHES..........

People will only remember about the money with Luca but
his problem was that he didn't know the terrain. He'd only
been in the Premier League, and the First Division, as it
was then, was almost a different game.

But I don't think anyone could dislike Luca. He's such
a lovely, lovely man. His natural instinct is just to be nice
to people. For someone so experienced and worldly-wise,
Luca really wore his heart on his sleeve. When we lost
games, I really felt for him, I really did.

He worked really hard. Ray used to tell me that Luca
would be watching videos of games all night, video after

video, so he put a hell of a lot into the job, but I think he found the league a difficult thing to adjust to.

## JUNE 2002
.........MORE DEPARTURES AT VICARAGE ROAD. LAST MONTH ELTON JOHN ENDED HIS 25-YEAR ASSOCIATION WITH THE CLUB AND NOW THEY HAVE SACKED GIANLUCA VIALLI AFTER JUST ONE SEASON IN CHARGE..........

Ray tipped me off and said, 'I think everyone's going to be sacked.' I thought I was going to get the sack with everyone else but they did it in reverse. They sacked Ray first, almost to force Luca out. But Luca stayed for a little while, bizarrely. For a while it looked like Luca was going to stay but eventually he went.

I got a phone call to say that the rest of the staff had been sacked. There were three of us left. Terry Byrne was kept on, Kevin Hitchcock, the goalkeeping coach, and me.

About a week after that, they said they were going to announce me as caretaker-manager for the summer, just to be here to keep things ticking over, which was fine by me.

## JULY 2002
.....MORE DEVELOPMENTS AT WATFORD. CARETAKER-MANAGER RAY LEWINGTON HAS BEEN APPOINTED ON A PERMANENT BASIS BY THE CLUB'S CHAIRMAN GRAHAM SIMPSON..........

Graham asked me if I wanted the job and I said okay, but then he wanted me to have an interview. I told him I wasn't going to do an interview because he knew who I was and what I did. He said the job was going to be a difficult one and that he owed it to me to explain. Then we went for a bizarre meeting with Barclays Bank.

They said that if I wanted the job, I had to buy into the fact that we could get the wage bill down from more than £10m [a year] to under £3m. I had to tell the Barclays Bank men that I knew what the job was and that I'd do it under those circumstances. I knew I might lose my reputation but I was happy to give it a bash anyway.

I knew I was going to have to release a lot of senior players but I don't think the senior players actually contributed too much to Luca's year. I wasn't particularly upset at losing a lot of them, and a lot of them were on ridiculously huge money. It wasn't as if I was trying to replace four or five top-class players. I was replacing four or five players that hadn't done well. I thought I could pick up some free transfers, and some loans in particular, and replace them. So I didn't think there'd be too much damage there.

The thing was that to reduce the wage bill by the amount we needed to, there was never going to be any respite. Every year it would be, right, 'We've got to chop this off, chop that off.' We looked to get half of the eight million off the wage bill in the first year. That was our aim.

Something that did make me laugh when I got the job was that I got a call from Oli Phillips. I didn't know him very well at the time but I liked him. He rang to offer his congratulations and then he told me that I'd got one per cent of the vote in a newspaper poll asking who the next manager should be. I told him that was probably my mum voting.

I knew I'd got the job because I was fairly cheap, because I was already there and because they didn't have to pay compensation to anyone, so it was convenient.

## SEPTEMBER 2002

## .....THE COLLAPSE OF ITV DIGITAL HAS PLUNGED MANY CLUBS INTO FINANCIAL TROUBLE. WATFORD HAVE ANNOUNCED THAT THEIR PLAYERS HAVE AGREED TO DEFER 12 PER CENT OF THEIR WAGES....

The chairman called me in and said we were going to be in trouble if we didn't do it. I wasn't on great money and I said, 'Is it just me?' He said, 'No, no, no, no. I'm talking about the squad.' I told him that wasn't going to go down well. He said: 'Listen, the numbers are worse than we thought. and if we don't do this, we go into administration and that's it. Finito.'

So we called a meeting with the boys. Someone from the PFA [the players' union] came down and at first there were a few in the squad who said, 'No, we're not doing it.' But a lot of them said 'If that's what it takes, we'll do it.'

Terry Byrne, who was director of football, did a great job with the lads. Eventually they were all persuaded, and we got a unanimous decision, but with the proviso that if we got any money that wasn't budgeted for, like if we sold someone for big money or went on a cup run, the club would use some of that money to pay the players back.

## .....FULL TIME AT BRAMALL LANE AND WATFORD HAVE PUT THEIR FINANCIAL WOES ASIDE TO WIN 2-1.........

The very next game was Sheffield United away. We were mid-table and doing quite well, and we won 2-1. The news had come out that the players were taking a wage cut to save the club and it was an amazing atmosphere. It was like we'd won the World Cup. That is probably as close as I've ever seen players and fans come together.

The fans were really, really happy that the squad had done this for their club. They really appreciated it and they created an atmosphere that helped the players win a very difficult game.

## APRIL 2003
## .....SO, IT WILL BE AN ALL-PREMIERSHIP FA CUP FINAL AT CARDIFF AFTER SOUTHAMPTON BEAT WATFORD 2-1 AT VILLA PARK.....

The semi-final whizzed by and I don't think we did ourselves justice. I didn't feel that we believed we had a chance and I think we were a bit limp. We started well, nice and bright, and Heidar Helguson should have scored, but after that we couldn't handle their extra quality. Southampton weren't a fantastically gifted side but they were better than us technically. There was no hard luck story; I just felt we could have done a little bit more.

We'd had such a good cup run, beating two Premier League sides – Sunderland and West Brom – and then Burnley without conceding a goal. I felt it could have been our year, so it was disappointing. Under the circumstances, I think the chairman would have settled for an FA Cup semi-final appearance before the season had started.

I'd had a massively difficult choice to make between Tommy Smith or Michael Chopra. Tommy was a very good player but he didn't score enough goals. Just before the semi-final, Michael, who was on loan from Newcastle, bagged four away at Burnley [in a 7-4 win], which is no mean feat, so I stuck him in.

I don't think Tom ever spoke to me again, actually, but as a manager you would expect that. I was going to go with Helguson and either Smith or Chopra. I was thinking, 'If I am honest, who is more likely to score a goal in a big game like this?' I thought it would be Chopra. Really, that was the end of Smithy. I don't think he wanted to hang about after that, but that's what managers have to do sometimes. I don't regret making that decision and I'd probably do the same thing tomorrow if I had the same choice. It seemed logical to me. Chopra's goalscoring record was fantastic in the reserves and at Newcastle.

## AUGUST 2003
.....BREAKING NEWS: MANCHESTER UNITED'S JIMMY DAVIS HAS BEEN KILLED IN A CAR ACCIDENT ON THE M40. THE 21-YEAR-OLD HAD RECENTLY JOINED WATFORD ON LOAN.....

It was the opening day of the season – a day I will never forget. I got a call from Terry Byrne saying there'd been an accident, and just to meet him at Vicarage Road quickly – that's all he said. So I got in the car and after ten minutes the phone went again, and Anne, my wife, was crying because Ray Harford, who'd been my mentor and one of my best mates in football, had just died the very same day.

Unbeknown to me, as I was driving in, someone had got their story mixed up that someone had died at Watford and it was not Ray Harford, but me. So it actually went out on a local radio station that I'd died in a car crash.

So I got in, a little bit choked up, and I was thinking, 'What's happened?' I wasn't expecting anyone else to have died. When I got out of the car, I saw Nigel Gibbs and he looked at me and nearly fainted because he'd been told I'd died.

Then I got into the office and Terry broke the news to me about Jimmy. The chairman was there and told me that they were going to get the game called off because the players were a mess. Paul Robinson was absolutely heartbroken, honestly, sobbing, and just could not stop.

All the lads had taken to Jim – he was one of those bubbly little characters, such a nice lad. I remember when he did his initiation song on his first day with the team. Usually they're a little bit shy and might sing a few verses, but Jim chose this song, and sang the whole lot, and wouldn't get off the table. The players were telling him to stop but he wouldn't. He just kept singing and Terry eventually got hold of him, slung him over his shoulders and took him out the room, and he was still singing. He was a lovely little kid.

Sir Alex Ferguson called me to ask what had happened. I told him that because Jimmy had been injured and wasn't going to play in the game, he'd gone home to see his mum, but I'd told him he had to be back to watch the match. He was only going an hour down the road. We'll never know what happened.

He'd always been good to me, Fergie. He had a reputation for helping out other managers. The previous year, he rang me up and asked if I wanted to meet at the Landmark Hotel in London for breakfast. He said he had one or two players he would like to go out on loan, and that he like the way I played football.

We were sitting together for three hours. He gave me a list of players that he would be happy to come to Watford and one of them was Jim. I took Danny Webber straight away. The only problem was the wages. Watford paid next to nothing for him. But that was the start of a really good relationship between the clubs. He really did look after us. However, after Jimmy died, I felt I couldn't go back to him again. It just didn't feel right.

## JANUARY 2005
.....WATFORD CHAIRMAN GRAHAM SIMPSON HAS HAILED MANAGER RAY LEWINGTON AFTER THE CLUB REACHED THE SEMI-FINAL OF THE CARLING CUP. THEY NOW HAVE TWO MONEY-SPINNING TIES AGAINST LIVERPOOL.......

We'd beaten Southampton and Portsmouth, two Premier League clubs, to reach the semi-final, and at the fans' forum the chairman kept patting me on the back and saying: 'We won't go down as long as Ray's here.' He said he'd never sack me. He always said that and, 'You've got a job here for life,' and, 'When the finances get better, we'll make sure that you're paid for what you've done for these three years.'

## MARCH 2005
........BREAKING NEWS: WATFORD HAVE SACKED MANAGER RAY LEWINGTON WITH SEVEN GAMES OF THE SEASON REMAINING..........

Oli Phillips phoned me late at night, about 11.30, and said: 'I hope I'm wrong but has the chairman been in touch with you? Because the rumour is that they are going to sack you.' I didn't tell Anne and went to bed. The next morning, the phone rang at 7.30 and I knew straight away. It was the chief executive, Mark Ashton. The day he walked into the club was the day I got sacked, effectively.

I went to see Ashton and the chairman, who gave the speech, 'This is the hardest thing I've ever had to do,' like they all do. He was worried that we would go down, and that we couldn't afford to. I was confident that we wouldn't go down, that we had got a buffer, and we'd finally sorted the reduction in the wage bill.

He said, 'I've got to make the decision.' Then he gave me an envelope. He told me to open it when I got out, or read it there but it was nothing special. Then I told him I'd go into the training ground to pick my stuff up, but he said I couldn't go there or to the ground. I wasn't allowed under the terms of the letter that I had in my hands. I said, 'So that's it?' He said, 'Yeah, afraid so.' So in the end I just took the letter so I could go. I just wanted to get out of there.

I felt a sense of injustice; I felt let down. If you're a manager and you come under pressure, and the crowd are booing, and you're in the bottom three, you almost expect it. I didn't expect to get the sack because we'd only just been in the semi-final and lost against Liverpool having played very well at Anfield, and made a bit of money for the club.

That was the worst thing. He didn't even give me the chance to get it right – we'd satisfied the bank, and now we could actually increase the overdraft a little bit, and there would be some money to spend – not only on transfer fees but on wages.

Coxy [Neil Cox] phoned me up and said he and the players wanted to meet, even if I couldn't come to the training ground. We went to a pub nearby and said our goodbyes over a pint. They asked me what had happened, and I said they sacked me because they thought we were going to go down. The players were all saying, 'We're not going to go down. How did they come to that one?'

It's the only time I've ever been sacked. The first two or three days after it happens, the phone doesn't stop with people ringing and being nice to you. In a way, that's the last thing you want. Then all of a sudden the phone calls stop and you're just left there thinking, 'What am I going to do now?'

## JULY 2005
### .....AHEAD OF THE NEW SEASON, FULHAM MANAGER CHRIS COLEMAN HAS ADDED RAY LEWINGTON TO HIS COACHING STAFF AT CRAVEN COTTAGE........

Chris called me up. I'd been his coach at Crystal Palace and he said that he wanted me in at Fulham. He wanted me to oversee things. He was happy with his best mate Steve Kean as his first team coach and he had some other younger coaches. He had told me that if something came up – a manager's job – then I could go. It was lovely – really good. The money was decent and it was great to feel wanted again.

I don't hold grudges, and I threw myself into the new job. I was angry for a few weeks when I started seeing all these players arrive at Watford, on big money, obviously. Then you just think to yourself, 'So what? Is it going to matter to me?' I'd got a nice job and Chris Coleman was fantastic. It's done, gone. I couldn't change what had happened, so I just had to forget it.

## MAY 2012
### .....BREAKING NEWS: RAY LEWINGTON HAS BEEN APPOINTED AS ROY HODGSON'S ASSISTANT WITH THE ENGLAND NATIONAL TEAM..........

Incredible. The national team! Roy is the most recognisable man in England, apart from the Prime Minister, maybe. The reaction of people to him is unbelievable and in the lead-up to the World Cup he was the focal point of the whole country. The scale of it – you can't comprehend what it's like – but he handles it fantastically well.

I think I'm happier in the background. I could be a manager tomorrow. If the opportunity came along, and I thought it was the right one for me, I'd do it, although while I've got this job, obviously not. It doesn't frighten me, management. I think I'm better suited as someone who can just get on.

Roy's fantastic with the media. I'm not – I tie up a little bit, and I don't particularly like all the things you have to do as a manager. The thing I like best is being on the pitch with the players – that's what I really enjoy – so I'm probably best suited for a number two or a coaching job, because that's what I enjoy.

I don't care about the money. What the managers are earning, they deserve because of all the pressure they're under. We're under nothing like the pressure of the manager. We all think that we care, and we do, but when you're the manager, the buck stops with you. All roads lead to you. It's difficult and you've really got to take that on board. At my stage of life now, I'm happier as a number two.

The players don't judge you, but they'll know if you can't do the job because there will be cracks in your armoury. I've got a lot of confidence in myself and in my coaching. It's what I love – what I do well. England players are probably easier to work with than a lot of club players, because they are the best. Technically, they are the best. They look after themselves and they're used to being the best. They're not the wannabes. The wannabes are the ones that give you trouble; they actually think they're better than they are. This lot are here. They don't have to prove anything else. They just work hard, do it properly.

# RONNY ROSENTHAL

**On almost joining Udinese in 1989**
'I met Mr Pozzo and we agreed
the transfer. Then I went on
holiday to Israel and I saw a
headline in the newspaper:
Rosenthal fails medical.'

## 8

Ronny Rosenthal was a key part of Graham Taylor's rebuilding plan in the summer of 1997.

Having played for Liverpool and Tottenham, he had experience at the top level.

His pace and trickery on the wing made him an immediate hit at Vicarage Road.

For a while, it seemed likely that Ronny's son, Tom, might follow in his footsteps at Watford.

But as Rosenthal's career shows, football can be a funny old game.

# RONNY ROSENTHAL

When I arrive at Ronny Rosenthal's home in Hampstead, north London, he's on the phone. He answers the door and ushers me into his office – a large room at the front of the house with a big bay window and an executive-style desk covered in piles of papers. I wait while he finishes his call and glance around the room. There are two large bookcases going up to the ceiling, both crammed with DVD cases – hundreds of discs showing football matches from all over the world.

Behind me are framed shirts that tell the story of Ronny Rosenthal's career, which spanned almost two decades from the end of the 1970s.

There's the green of his first club, Maccabi Haifa, the blue and black of Club Brugge, the reds of Liverpool and Standard Liège, the white of Tottenham and the Israeli national team, and finally the yellow of Watford.

The Watford shirt of Rosenthal's time was a simple and stylish design with a wide vertical red stripe on one side and the CTX logo, belonging to the computer monitor manufacturer that sponsored the club.

I notice something is awry with Rosenthal's display. The Standard Liège and Liverpool shirts are in the wrong order.

'That was my wife's idea,' he says with a smile when he finishes his call. 'She said that if I put them in the right order, the Liverpool shirt would be hidden when the door is open.'

What about Standard Liège? Does he not want to

remember his time there? 'No, no, it's not that…' he says. 'I met my wife in Liège, so I have a reminder every day.'

Rosenthal has every reason to remember his time at Anfield fondly. Many would no doubt bring up the famous 'miss' at Villa Park in 1992, when he rounded the keeper and had the goal at the Holte End to his mercy but managed to hit the bar from about ten yards.

Indeed, when I get around to asking him about it, he is in surprisingly good humour. 'The miss!' he says in mock horror. 'No! No! Everyone asks about it but I do not let things like this haunt me. It's part of the game. If you don't want to miss, don't play football. The player that does not make a mistake does not exist.'

Instead, Rosenthal prefers to make the point that he was part of the last Liverpool team to win the league title, coming up for quarter of a century ago now. He joined them on loan from Standard Liège just before the transfer deadline in March 1990, scored a hat-trick on his full debut and finished up with seven goals in eight games. Liverpool is also where his oldest son, Dean, was born.

At Anfield, he teamed up with former Watford winger John Barnes as they denied Graham Taylor's Aston Villa the title. In fact, Taylor tried to block Rosenthal's transfer, according to Rosenthal.

'When I joined Liverpool, Graham was leading the table with Aston Villa and I think he asked the FA why Liverpool were allowed to sign another foreign player because there were rules about how many foreign players each team could have. Liverpool said they had some injuries… Anyway, I signed just before the five o'clock transfer deadline but the fax from the Belgian FA came afterwards and I don't think Graham was too happy about it. Anyway, when he signed me for Watford, he joked that I cost him the championship.'

* * *

Rosenthal joined Watford towards the end of his career. By August 1997 he was just a couple of months shy of his 34th birthday. Graham Taylor knew that Rosenthal's pace and experience would be an asset in the Second Division and although he knew he probably wouldn't last the distance, Taylor offered a three-year contract.

The transfer happened relatively late in the summer after being mooted by Brian Anderson, one of the directors who was part of the new consortium that bought the club from Jack Petchey.

'A friend of mine knew Brian Anderson. He told Brian that I was free. I have to be honest, at that time I was not thinking of going from the Premier League to the Second Division but the other thing was that I did not want to move out of London. I met Graham and he said that he had a group of very young, hungry players but he needed an experienced one,' says Rosenthal. 'He told me he liked my style of game – you know, someone who can make things happen. I wasn't going to kid myself that I could run like I did three or four years before but I thought I could have an impact in that division.'

At Rosenthal's first training session, Taylor told him – in front of all the other players – that he'd substitute him if he crossed the halfway line into his own half. 'Ronny is very good at a lot of things,' Taylor said. 'But he's not a defender.'

Rosenthal laughs. 'Yes, I remember that. It was a joke but he wanted me to be in the other half of the pitch where I could score goals rather than chasing back.'

Undoubtedly his finest moment came in a home game against Blackpool on November 1, 1997. Richard Johnson had the ball on the halfway line, over on the left-hand side of the pitch. He turned inside and touched the ball to Rosenthal, who took it in his stride, just inside the Blackpool half. Surging forward he ran between two defenders and past a third, whose desperate lunge was far too late. Rosenthal was already through and about to enter the penalty area. As the goalkeeper came out to narrow the angle Rosenthal shaped as if to unleash a powerful shot only to lift the ball deftly, delicately, over the keeper's sliding body and into the net at the Rookery end.

Not surprisingly, it won Rosenthal the goal of the season award.

'Yes, yes,' he says, a grin just about breaking out. 'I remember it. A nice goal...'

Nice? It was better than nice, Ronny.

* * *

Rosenthal was born in Haifa, Israel, in 1963. His parents were immigrants. His father was born in Romania and his mother was born in Morocco. 'Israel was still a new country,' he says. 'We are talking about 15 years after the independence of Israel, and Jewish people were coming from all over the world to live there. From a young age, I heard different languages – my father spoke Romanian, my mother spoke French. My dad had already been in Israel since about 1950 and my mum came ten years after that. They met in 1962 and I was born in 1963. My mum did not speak a word of Hebrew so they spoke in French at the beginning.

'My father opened a modest jewellery shop because his brother was in the business. Before that he'd been a taxi driver and he'd worked in a bank but he didn't want to be employed by someone else, he wanted his own freedom. It was a very modest upbringing. I wouldn't say poor but I definitely wouldn't say rich.'

At school, Rosenthal excelled at athletics – sprinting and

long jump particularly – but football was not played at school. The family moved to an apartment right next to Maccabi Haifa's new stadium. Rosenthal turns the screen on his desk towards me, calls up Google Maps and takes me on a virtual tour of Haifa, scrolling through the images until he spots his apartment, just on the hillside opposite the football ground.

Maccabi Haifa were overshadowed by the city's other team, Hapoel, and by the bigger clubs in Tel Aviv at the time but Rosenthal and his father would go to games because the stadium was a short walk away.

'Saturday is the day of rest – like Sunday in England,' he says. 'But Saturday was also the day for football. We were not a religious family, I didn't go to synagogue, so Saturday was all about football. Football in Israel was created by immigrants from European countries so they played on Saturdays and I think perhaps the Jewish people who came from Europe were a bit less religious than the Jewish people from the Middle East.'

Rosenthal started playing football in the street with his friends, then joined the Maccabi club when he was ten, although there were no organised leagues for children until they reached the age of 12.

It was an idyllic upbringing. Haifi, with its sunshine, beaches and whitewashed architecture, looks like the south of France. Although security has always been a consideration in Israel, Rosenthal remembers a peaceful upbringing, although not without one or two incidents.

'I was almost ten when the Yom Kippur War happened in 1973,' he says. 'Yom Kippur to Jewish people is like Christmas Day. Egypt and Syria decided to stage an attack on the day of Yom Kippur because they knew that the defences at the border would be at a minimal level. I was walking down near the beach and I saw helicopters landing near the big hospital with all the injured soldiers. But I never felt under threat. I never heard a bomb explode near me. It was a very quiet childhood.'

Football soon came to dominate Rosenthal's life once he joined Maccabi Haifa. The first team were relegated from Israel's top flight and Rosenthal got the opportunity to make his debut when he was still 16. 'We were losing 1-0 to a team called Kiryat-Shmona. I came on and scored two goals and we won the game.'

Maccabi got back into the First Division and in 1983-84, the season Rosenthal turned 20, they were in the hunt for their first league title. 'It was May 1984 and we had been on a fantastic run. We won eight in a row but the team at the top, Beitar Jerusalem, didn't drop any points until the unexpectedly lost a game and we went to the top of the table with one game remaining,' he says.

Their last game was at home. A win would make history for the club. 'We stayed in a hotel the night before a game,' he says. 'We never did that normally but did so because it was such an important game. From the hotel, we could see the fans heading to the stadium. Five hours before kick-off, it was full with 28,000 fans.'

Maccabi Haifa beat Maccabi Tel Aviv 1-0 to clinch their first championship and they defended their title the following year. They almost won it for a third time in 1986. Maccabi needed a draw in their final game against Hapoel Tel Aviv, their closest challengers. 'We should have won the league weeks before but it went down to the last game and there was a huge mistake from the referee ten minutes from the end,' he says. 'They scored a goal that was offside and they won. The referee was from the Tel Aviv area…'

Rosenthal had proved himself in Israel and knew that to progress his career he would have to leave. At the time, Israeli clubs did not play in the European Cup or the Uefa Cup, and, although he was an international, the chances to test himself against better defences were few and far between. An Israeli who lived in Belgium had recommended Rosenthal to Club Brugge. Although he was not convinced initially, Rosenthal made the move and within a couple of seasons Club Brugge had won the Belgian league and reached the semi-finals of the Uefa Cup.

After two successful years in the Flemish-speaking part of Belgium, he was transferred across the 'border' to Standard Liège in the French-speaking region.

'Brugge were interested in a young player at Standard Liège and Standard didn't want to sell him, so the only way they could do the deal was if I went to Liège,' he says. 'The funny thing is, Brugge had to pay money and give me away, so it wasn't such a great transfer for them. I ended up being top-scorer for Standard Liège so it was a big disaster for Brugge.'

The transfer to Liège worked out perfectly for more than one reason. The day before his first training session with his new club, Rosenthal arrived at the stadium to pick up his kit and some other things and as he walked across the car park a woman was walking in the opposite direction.

'That was the first time I saw Nancy,' he says. 'She worked for the commercial department at the club. If Club Brugge had not sold me, I would not have met the most beautiful girl in Belgium.'

* * *

The football world is a place of connections and coincidences. Players are bought and sold, and as they criss-cross Europe and the world, they brush past each other and move on. Rosenthal's career almost took him to Udinese in Italy, which was owned by Giampaolo Pozzo, now owner of Watford. In 1989, after a year with Standard Liège, Rosenthal actually signed for the

Italian club. 'It was in May, at the end of the season,' he says. 'I met Mr Pozzo and we agreed the transfer, subject to the results of a medical. The transfer fee was a million dollars, around £600,000, so a lot of money then. I went on holiday to Israel and then a couple of weeks before I was due to go to Udine, I saw a headline in the newspaper: "Rosenthal fails medical."

'I'd had the medical but they hadn't said anything so I assumed that everything was okay. Now, I was born with a minor abnormality in my back but it had never been a problem before.'

Rosenthal believes two things happened to put Udinese off. 'They signed an Argentinian player called Abel Balbo. Italian clubs could only have three foreign players at the time and I think they decided they wanted Balbo, who was younger than me. Also, the newspaper reported that some anti-Semitic graffiti had been found on a wall at the stadium saying something like, "We don't want a Jew here." I don't know if that was true but that's what the paper said.'

He played the bulk of the season at Standard Liège and then, in early 1990, he found himself at Kenilworth Road, home of Luton Town.

'I had a trial there,' he says. 'Alec Chamberlain, who I later played with at Watford, was their goalkeeper. I went there and played for the reserves and the manager, Jim Ryan, wanted to take me but Luton couldn't afford the money. Standard Liège wanted £500,000. Then I went to Hibs in Scotland for a couple of days. Then Liverpool invited me for a trial. Kenny Dalglish had spoken to Jim Ryan, who told him about me, and so I ended up going there on loan.'

After scoring a glut of goals to secure the title for Liverpool, he signed permanently in the summer. Although this coincided with the decline of the great Anfield dynasty, Rosenthal enjoyed his time there, although he believes that Graeme Souness, who followed Dalglish as manager, recruited too many players who were not up to Liverpool's high standards. Their scouting network, once one of the finest, stopped finding the gems.

\* \* \*

That takes us neatly on to the subject of the tower of DVDs in Rosenthal's office. He describes himself as a football consultant these days, and his work involves spotting talented players who could offer value-for-money to the top clubs in England.

'I don't know if you noticed,' he says, 'but I have four satellite dishes on the top of my roof so I can watch football from all over the world. I look for good players but I try to match them to clubs who need a certain type of player.'

When he was at Watford, Rosenthal recommended Michel Ngonge, the Belgian-born Congolese striker who had played for several clubs in Belgium before joining Samsunspor in Turkey. He also suggested Graham Taylor look at Alon Hazan, the cultured Israeli midfielder who added a calming influence at vital moments during two hectic promotion run-ins.

'Seeing a top player is one thing but to understand how to fit a club to the player is a completely different business,' he says before listing some of those he had a hand in bringing to the Premier League. 'Dimitar Berbatov, Gilberto Silva, Fréderic Kanoute... I discovered Vincent Kompany and I suggested him to a couple of clubs but they couldn't see it at the time.' Belgium is a fertile market, Rosenthal says, because the players can be picked up cheaply while they are there. 'I recommended Moussa Dembélé, who went to Tottenham [for £15million], when he was still in Belgium but clubs prefer to wait and then pay a huge amount of money to buy the player later rather than when he is cheap.'

The internet has made it easier for Rosenthal to do his job.

He has access to a huge database of players from all over the world. He opens it up on his screen and clicks on the Watford squad, opens up a player's file and scrolls through a list of information that makes the Football Manager computer game look basic. Rosenthal is a freelancer. He doesn't work for specific clubs or players – he tries to match one to the other and he takes a sort of finder's fee if a transfer comes off.

What does Rosenthal think of the Pozzo family, who own Udinese, Watford and Granada in Spain? They have a scouting network that spans the world and their own pool of more than 100 players. In a way, they've cut out the middle men like Rosenthal, and are doing the legwork themselves. Their model is very similar – spot players when they are cheap, develop them and sell them for a good profit. Their record, with Udinese particularly, is impressive, although it might be a little too much of a scattergun approach for some Watford supporters.

Rosenthal opens up the Watford page on his database and hovers the cursor over the players' names, offering his verdicts as he goes. 'I haven't seen enough of the first team to be able to tell you more than you already know, but there are some I like. Forestieri is a very good player but maybe he's better as a winger and not a main striker – I don't know. Anya is very good but I think he is better on the right side. Then you need someone on the left who can do the same thing. Pudil is a nice player but you don't get the same contribution; he does not have the same element of surprise that Anya can give. So the team becomes a little bit unbalanced. But look, I have not seen enough of them to say for sure.'

He begins to scroll through the names of some of the younger players. 'Nice player but not enough pace. With his skill he could play for a top club one day but he hasn't got the pace,' he says of one young Watford player. 'No, I don't think he will make it,' he says of another.

Of course, football is a game of opinions and Rosenthal has a vested interest – at least he did at the time we met to do this interview. His younger son, Tom, was one of the shining lights in the Watford youth team. Ronny was looking forward to seeing his son play against Liverpool in the FA Youth Cup. Watford lost the fifth round tie at Vicarage Road 2-0 but the younger Rosenthal's development suggested that he might follow in his father's footsteps and pull on the yellow shirt for the first team. However, shortly after the start of the new season, Rosenthal Jnr moved to Zulte Waregem in the Belgian First Division.

As the conversation switches to the subject of his son, Rosenthal turns to the computer screen again and calls up a succession of YouTube clips of Tom playing for the Belgian under-18 team. 'That's him,' he says, indicating the tallest player on the pitch. 'He's very comfortable on the ball, he's a midfield player but he can play in an offensive role or a defensive one.'

We watch another clip of Tom running from deep, past several opposition defenders. Ronny mutters his own commentary quietly as we watch. 'Past one… two... three… little dummy… four… five… then the goal,' he says.

'When the Israeli television station discovered this clip they played it but with commentary from one of the best goals I scored in my career for Israel.'

At 6ft 2, Tom Rosenthal is a few inches taller than his dad and as he runs he is more upright than his dad was. It's not just pride in his son's ability that makes Rosenthal believe he can make it.

'Tom has always been tall for his age but now he is developing pace,' he says. 'I was explosive and I think he can achieve a little bit of that.

'He didn't have a chance to play for the first team at Watford. I think that in another system he would have had a chance already. Zulte Waregem said he would get a chance to play in the first team. It's a great opportunity to play senior football. He plays for the Belgian under-18s – he has a Belgian passport – so it's a good move for him.'

Perhaps it will be a case of Watford's loss and Waregem's gain? Time will tell.

\* \* \*

Rosenthal's pace earned him the nickname 'Rocket Ronny' and his popularity spawned an upbeat song, which you'll now be singing to yourself if you remember it.

(Ronny, oh Ronny Ronny, oh Ronny Ronny, oh Ronny Rosen-thal. Hey!)

He was the very definition of an impact player and he was often deployed as a substitute by Liverpool and Tottenham. At Watford, he made an immediate impression – coming on as sub in a League Cup tie at Swindon Town and scoring in the 2-0 win. He wasn't prolific, although a return of 11 goals in 31 appearances in his first season was far from shabby, particularly considering he had two spells on the sidelines with injury. His contribution was more significant, he says.

'I tried to be a coach on the pitch. I would talk to the players, try to encourage them and motivate them and help them be successful because I wasn't coming to Watford just to pick up my wages and go home.

'When I signed for Watford, we had agreed on everything but I asked for a bonus if we went up to the First Division. I think the bonus was £80,000. Then I said, "Okay, but what about a bonus if we go up to the Premier League?" Graham Taylor and John Alexander [the club secretary] looked at each other but I was serious. I said, "Look, I think we can go up to the Premier League in two years and if we do I think that's worth a bonus, no?" I was on a Premier League salary at Tottenham and I was agreeing to come down two divisions.'

Watford won the Second Division title in 1998 and Rosenthal played a key role. He helped destroy Luton Town 4-0 at Kenilworth Road, taking every opportunity to run at the hapless Hatters defence. He scored that goal of the season against Blackpool.

Although he started the following season in the team, he suffered another injury. At the age of 35, the injuries were starting to take their toll. He battled back, played a few reserve games – 'We played our reserve matches at Northwood, where the pitch was not very pleasant to play on when it was muddy,' he says – and then, in a rare display of what might be called sentimentality, Graham Taylor put Rosenthal on the bench for the FA Cup third round tie against Tottenham at White Hart Lane.

Rosenthal came on at half-time, with the Hornets trailing 4-2 having taken a first-minute lead. He got a rousing reception from the home fans, as well as the travelling Watford supporters. 'It was a very nice gesture by Graham to let me play in that game because I had been out for a few months and I was not properly fit. It was a nice way to stop my career.'

Although he made only one more appearance, against West Brom, he was still around the place as Watford reached the play-offs.

'I really enjoyed seeing the team achieve something. The players were improving very quickly and I was very happy to see that they would get a chance to play in the Premier League.

At Wembley, he sat on the bench with the other squad members and he celebrated as heartily as those who had played in the game.

'I should say, I didn't get my bonus for reaching the Premier League because it was subject to me playing 60 or 70 per cent of the game. Graham Taylor was careful with the club's money,' he says, laughing.

'That summer, Graham helped me to retire, shall we say. He was right. I was not giving to the club any more. The injuries were coming more often. I had one year left on my contract but we agreed a way for me to retire. I bought this house when I retired,' he adds.

Dean and Tom were still children. Both of them were football mad and it struck me that the spacious back garden of their house in Hampstead was a good place to grow up. There's room for a couple of five-a-side goals and there's a ball suspended from a post so they could practice heading.

They spent hours out there and both showed early promise, although Dean has followed his father into the football business while Tom progressed through the academy system at Watford before moving to Belgium.

For a while it seemed like Tom might be the next player to progress through the youth system and make it as a first team player at Watford. Ronny believes he has a chance to make it if he can continue the curve of improvement he's shown over the past couple of years.

Tom qualifies for three countries – Israel and Belgium, the countries of his parents, and England, the country of his birth. He opted to play for Belgium at under-18 level, although Israel have also expressed an interest.

'It's his choice,' says Rosenthal. 'It's important he makes the best decision for his career and Belgium have a very good reputation for developing young players. You only have to look at the number of Belgian players who have come to the Premier League to see that.'

Although the chances of seeing another Rosenthal in a yellow shirt have receded, Ronny's career proves that in football anything can happen.

Whatever happens in the future, the Rosenthal name will always been remembered fondly, if only for that goal against Blackpool, which revived memories of the greatest wingplay Hornets fans had ever witnessed. Watford have always enjoyed the sight of a winger who is able to send defenders into a spin. Stewart Scullion and John Barnes were arguably the finest, but Rosenthal was not that far behind them.

# THE HOLDSWORTHS

**Who was the better player?**
'David was just a centre-half. He couldn't tell me about flair, could he?'
**Dean Holdsworth**

'Me, because he was just a goalscorer. I could do more than that.'
**David Holdsworth**

## 9

David Holdsworth entered the world 40 minutes before his twin brother Dean. Sixteen years later they signed for Watford.

Although they looked very similar, they had very different characters and careers. David was a tough-tackling, no-nonsense defender; Dean played at the opposite end of the pitch and thrived on scoring goals.

Dean had to move on to get his career going while David stayed and gave a decade of loyal service to the Hornets.

Here they go head-to-head once again to talk about their time at Vicarage Road and beyond.

# DAVID & DEAN HOLDSWORTH

As Watford walked out under Wembley's twin towers in 1984, another identical pair of twins were walking into Vicarage Road. The FA Cup Final defeat to Everton may have marked a disappointing end of the road for the first team in north-west London, but at around the same time two brothers from the north-east of the capital signed as apprentices.

David and Dean Holdsworth had been recruited as schoolboys from their home in Woodford. They came as a package, on the order of their mother, but they would go on to lead very different careers at the club and beyond.

The signs were there from the very beginning that they had contrasting traits. David was the tough-tackling defender, eager to be first into any challenge, while Dean, whose goals grabbed the attention, was fashionably late even on the day of their birth because he was 'laid back and waited to see what life was like on the outside', as he puts it.

Their tale after that is of hard knocks on and off the field. They had a tough upbringing: their father was not on the scene and they were sometimes moved into temporary housing. Guidance was needed and they found it at Vicarage Road under the influence of Tom Walley – the strict disciplinarian who ran Watford's youth system in the 1980s.

Despite being quite different characters, they each found a way to make it in the game. They helped Watford reach the FA Youth Cup final in 1985, when they went down to a Newcastle side inspired by Paul Gascoigne in the second leg at Vicarage Road. Among their contemporaries in the Watford youth team were Iwan Roberts and Malcolm Allen, who went on to play in the top flight and for the Welsh national team, Tim Sherwood, who won a Premier League title with Blackburn, and, later, David James, who kept goal for Liverpool and England.

Dean made his Watford debut first, against Luton in December 1987, but quickly found the path led him away from the club. After loan spells at Carlisle, Port Vale, Swansea and Brentford, he was sold to the west London club for £125,000 in September 1989. Steve Harrison, the Watford manager who agreed the transfer, later admitted that was a mistake and so it proved because Holdsworth top-scored for Brentford as they achieved promotion to the Second Division (now the Championship) a couple of seasons later.

His goals earned him a move to Wimbledon in the Premier League and he became a fully-fledged member of the Crazy Gang, although he added to the glamour with his model looks and the model girlfriend.

In contrast, David stuck with Watford and earned a call-up for the England under-21 team. There were highs – he scored one of the goals as Watford knocked the champions, Leeds United, out of the League Cup in November 1992 – but the club was on a downward trend.

A couple of years later he formed a formidable partnership with Colin Foster, occasionally playing at the heart of a three-man formation that also featured Keith Millen, as Watford established themselves as one of the meanest defences in the league. But following relegation to the third tier in 1996, it was time to move on.

After more than 300 appearances in a Watford shirt he might have expected a fonder farewell. He joined Sheffield United and missed out on promotion to the Premier League when they were beaten by Crystal Palace in the play-off final at Wembley. In fact, the play-offs were to prove his nemesis. He lost out in the play-offs five seasons in a row – twice with the Blades and three times with Birmingham City. In 1999, he was sent off in the semi-final second leg against Watford as the Hornets hung on before winning on penalties and going on to reach the Premier League.

The twins met each other on the pitch several times during their careers, with each challenge between them having the added spice of a sibling rivalry. They even faced each other as managers – the first time twins had gone head-to-head in the dugout at a match in England's top five divisions – when Dean was in charge of Newport County and David was at Mansfield Town in the Conference.

They have lived many miles apart for much of their lives and, at times, have been divided by more than distance. Here they unite to deal with the key issues of their lives and careers, with and without each other. And we find that the bond between them, the sense of mischievousness and the almost sixth sense twins seem to share is as strong as ever.

## THE HOLDSWORTH BROTHERS ON...
## GROWING UP FAST IN WOODFORD

**David:** We experienced things that you wouldn't want children to experience. Bless her, our mother – she really did have to work hard, and at times she was very ill. We had to fend for ourselves and certainly look after our younger sister. Much of the time we were on our own. A lot of people don't know what it's like having salad cream sandwiches for dinner or living on a council estate full of drunks and drug addicts.

When we reached secondary school, we never went. We used to go and work in a solicitor's office and run errands for a fiver a day. It was fantastic. What were we going to learn at

school? Learn how to fight and learn how to not do things.
We weren't academic.

Our senior school, Woodbridge, was right next to our
council estate and it was a tough school. I went to school for
two things: football and to have a punch-up. I look back at
them days and you had to fight back or you'd get beaten up.
But we had some great friends.

At home, the door was always open. Everybody used to
muck in together. Our mum was a keen darts player and we
spent a lot of our time in pubs watching her play. We didn't
get brought up eating healthily: we ate kebabs, Chinese and
pie and mash. That was the lifestyle that we had. You wouldn't
do it to kids now, goodness me. You just wouldn't think of
it. That was what we knew as the norm and we didn't know
anything else.

**Dean:** We spent a lot of our time living with grandparents
and my mum, depending on where we were staying or what
housing we were in and the size of the housing, but we had
our good days. We were strong together, with my nan and
grandad, which was fantastic. I remember sharing the same
house with three other families. We were in one room
together, and sharing a bathroom and kitchen. Those were the
tough times. We thought we were lucky when we got our own
place. Those early years were tough for my mum, looking after
three children on her own.

We never thought about sport. We thought about where we
would be living for the next period of our life. I always said we
lived in the penthouse on Broadmead estate as we were on the
top floor. You could compare dinners with the people in the
flats opposite, because you could see across to them.

It just gives you layers of character, doesn't it? You know,
if it doesn't really hurt you long-term then you remember it
and you say, 'Well, you can get by.' You're resilient aren't you?

## THEIR ABSENT FATHER

**Dean:** I never saw my dad for probably 17 years after he left. When I had a son myself – Bradley – I got in touch with my dad and said, 'You've got a grandson.' Everybody's got a story. We had a difficult time and in those days the laws were different. Sometimes, if the wife left, the children got put into sheltered housing, which we did. It was a tough time.

**David:** I love my dad. I just wish he'd been there. It wasn't nice, not having a dad. We were put in awful places. But bless her, my mum, she always did her best. We are very grateful for what she did then.

I wouldn't dream of not seeing my kids the way my dad did. Marriages fall down – that happens. It's hard when you've been away from someone for that time. I was pleased my brother did get in touch with him. There's no good being bitter and twisted. Life is life and you've got to deal with it. Sometimes it throws up hurdles. It made us what we were, in some ways.

## JOINING WATFORD

**Dean:** My mum did the negotiations. We were playing for Essex in a county match. I'd scored, Dave had played well and this little fella called Ken Brooks, who was a scout at the time and lived in Woodford Green, came knocking on the door. I'll never forget it. He said, 'I want to sign the lads,' and she said, 'They come together – they're a package.'

**David:** I was prepared to do that. I mean, I could have gone to West Ham or Arsenal, but he's my brother so we went to Watford together.

## LIVING IN DIGS IN GARSTON

**Dean:** That was an experience. On a Friday night our landlady would go out to bingo and they used to leave us a microwave dinner, but it was horrendous mashed potato in a microwave-able dish. We used to stick it in a carrier bag and throw it over the A41. And one night we forgot to throw it out and left it on the side in the bag. They didn't speak to us for about a week. It was very much that you lived in your bedroom rather than in their house. It became awkward because they were elderly. My mum or friends would ring up and they'd say, 'Oh, no, they're not in at the moment,' when we were. The phone was downstairs with a lock on it. They didn't trust us – that sort of thing. But it was painful; it was horrible really. We were away from home at 16 and getting treated like that.

**David:** She was a lovely lady, but I didn't care: it was crap food. I'm sorry – I don't mean to be rude to her but she couldn't cook. Stewed apple and squirty cream on top was not what I wanted. We wanted a kebab or crisps. I had a girlfriend and the best thing about her was she worked in a Wimpy on a Friday night. She was a little bit older and lovely-looking and I charmed my way into finding out how we could get free Wimpys.

We'd go over there and I'd give her a little wink and she'd come over with loads of food and we'd sit there and munch our way through it. We knew we weren't going to have stewed apples and crap like that on a Friday.

We would put our landlady's microwaveable dinner in a bag and we'd have a competition to see who could throw it the furthest, which is terrible really because it was going onto the dual carriageway. We could have hit people's cars and caused no end of accidents but I don't think we thought of the consequences.

There was that time we put it in a bag, left it on the side, fell asleep and forgot to throw it out. The bag of food was still sitting there when she got back from bingo. We came down stairs and her face was like stone.

## LIFE AS APPRENTICES

**Dean:** I had to clean Luther [Blissett] and [John] Barnesy's boots. It was good to get the players who had the most money because they'd give you a bigger tip at Christmas. Barnesy used to look after us. He'd give me a pair of his old Diadora boots if I was lucky. Sometimes the senior players would leave their washbags in the dressing room and we'd use their aftershave. It was like, 'What are we wearing tonight boys?'

Those days as apprentices were brilliant. There'd be 12 of us on a Friday afternoon having tag-team wrestling fights. It was good fun. Mad.

## TOM WALLEY

**Dean:** He was our youth team coach and he was one of the toughest men I've ever met in terms of discipline. I still think now that if I rung him up he'd frighten me. He was brilliant for us but he wouldn't get away with some of it now.

He'd make us pick chewing gum out of the carpet, or clean the toilets, or sweep the terraces, or do some painting. We were scared to fail because he was so disciplined.

We did a cross-country race in Cassiobury Park, and on the last hill I was about 30 yards ahead of Barnesy, who was a brilliant runner. In the last 100 yards, Tom said: 'If you don't win this, you're going to do it again.'

I was running, crying and praying that Barnesy didn't over-take me because if he had Tom would have made me do the whole run again. I won that because I was that frightened of him. He taught me the basics – the foundations of discipline and what it meant to be professional. Once you were a pro, he would treat you differently.

**David:** We didn't want to let Tom down, but he was trying to mould us all. And he was right. He was trying to mould us into what he wanted us to be. You know what? You'd work

hard to repay his faith. He'd still have a go at you. A lot of
players couldn't take him because he was too strong, but we'd
had him since we were 12. We knew he was a lunatic, but you
know what? He was a great man. A proper man.

**Dean:** Everywhere you went it felt like you had Tom's radar
on you. He was like the Predator: you could feel him somewhere in the trees, looking at you. You were so scared.
Whatever went on anywhere in Watford, Graham Taylor knew
about it – he had spies everywhere.

There was one incident on a Friday evening, which to this
day I have never told him about. It was one of the most
horrendous moments of my life. We were at home and it
wasn't late, but David had gone to see his girlfriend. The
phone went in the hallway, and my mum answered it.

She said: 'Tom's on the phone,' so I took the handset.

He said: 'Who's this?'

– It's Dean, Tom.

– What are you doing?

– Well, I'm in bed. I've got a game tomorrow.

– Where's David?

– He's in bed, asleep.

– Go and get him – I want to talk to him.

I was shaking but I went halfway up the stairs and
shouted, 'David,' so Tom could hear me. Then I got back on
the phone, and, in a muffled voice, like I'd just been woken up,
said: 'Hello, Tom, it's David.'

He swore at me about ten times and said: 'This is Deano.'

I said: 'No, no, it's not, it's Dave, Tom.'

He said: 'Go and get Deano.'

So I shout out, 'Dean, Tom wants you!' I take the phone
and say in my normal voice: 'Hello Tom.'

He said: 'I'm telling you this is Deano.'

'Well, you said you wanted to speak to me,' I replied. He

was a bit confused now so he said: 'Go and fucking get David again.'

'He's gone back to bed, Tom.'

'Just get him.'

So I had to go through the whole scenario again about five times, pretending to be David, then being me again, and in the end he said: 'I am going to fucking have you both tomorrow for this.'

**David:** I was at this girl's house – Nicola was her name – and I'm keeping an eye on my watch and I said: 'It's quarter to – I've got to be home by ten.' But it was a cuddle, and cuddles sometimes take a bit longer, don't they? It was a good couple of miles to our house from the council estate where this girl lived, so I started to run home because I knew I was going to be late and I knew Tom would ring at ten o'clock. I was running like the wind, sweating because it's all uphill, but I got home at bang on ten o'clock.

All I can hear is hysterics. I can hear both my mum and Dean saying: 'Oh my God, oh my God.'

'What's happened?' I ask.

They're both dying with laughter but my brother has got fear in his eyes. He told me what had happened and I laughed but he said: 'We are going to be in trouble tomorrow.'

As I walked in the door the next morning I got a massive smack round the head.

'Hey, you little bastard! I know it wasn't you on the phone,' says Tom.

'It was me! It was,' I said.

'No it wasn't. You're lying.'

'Honestly, it was me.'

'No it wasn't. I know your voice Holdsworth. If I ever find out it wasn't you, I will fucking kill you.'

I told Graham Taylor about it years later and he laughed.

## ELTON JOHN

**Dean:** He came in the gym once and I was doing sit-ups with
a medicine ball – 500 sit-ups we'd do. It was like pulling teeth
but you had to do them. Elton came through the door
wearing a pinstripe suit and a Trilby hat with a pink ponytail
and said: 'What you doing?'

I said: 'I'm doing sit-ups – what do you think I'm doing?'

He said: 'I'll have a go at them.'

So he got on the floor with his pinstripe suit on and started
doing them with his luminous pink ponytail flying around. I
kept throwing the medicine ball really hard in his stomach. He
only did about four or five, then he said, 'Cor that's bloomin'
tough.'

He would throw parties at his house in Windsor for
everyone at the club but the apprentices and younger pros
weren't allowed to drink. Elton knew that me, Tim Sherwood
and David James liked a bit of a night out, so we did talk to
him every now and then.

He got me a membership to Brown's nightclub in London
and said: 'Don't tell the gaffer.'

## GRAHAM TAYLOR

**David:** I needed a father-figure, because I was a bit of a
rogue, if you like. The only two people that have really tamed
me were Tom Walley and Graham Taylor. I phoned Graham
when I was about 34 or 35. I was reserve team manager at
Gretna and I had a young kid there who was a little rogue.
He'd been caught taking drugs up in Glasgow but, instead
of telling him he'd been a naughty boy, I put my arm around
him and said: 'Look, I've experienced some of the things that
you're going through and I'd like to give you support. We'll get
you the right support.'

I was thinking about it as I was driving home and I realised that Graham Taylor was probably the person who had helped me most. I was the naughty little boy who didn't care about anything. As you get older and wiser you realise you can't take on the world.

I rang Graham to thank him because the discipline he'd given me I was now passing on. We had a great conversation and I've had many more since with Graham.

When I became Lincoln manager, he was the first person I rang, partly because I knew he'd started at Lincoln, and I said: 'Please, come up any time.'

But nobody gave me more rollockings than Graham Taylor. I remember buying an MG convertible and he absolutely slaughtered me. He tore me to bits: 'You little flash bastard!' He was absolutely right but I was cock-a-hoop. I was a kid and I was only learning how to make mistakes.

I had a haircut once, and I had this ridiculous tram-line in the side of my head. Graham hammered me for that too: 'Get that thing out of your head! Get it cut!' As I was sat there, I was filling up. I was fearless of everyone else but I was so scared of him. And rightly so. He was a dictator. And I understand why. He is a control freak.

On the club's tour to China, I went along as the skip boy, to carry the kit and run errands and Elton was talking to me about Graham, and he said he was ruthless, and he was right.

Graham doesn't get enough credit for making it to the top in England. He gave me the discipline I needed and I fully respect him for that.

## DAVE BASSETT

**Dean:** Harry [everyone called Dave Bassett Harry] really loved me. He saw me playing behind the centre-forward in that sort of number ten role. He said: 'This is your role – you can get the ball and run at people.'

Harry was good to me but he was like a spaceman who had just landed in Watford. The ghost of Graham Taylor was still there. He had a totally different philosophy and, for those of us who were used to Graham's methods, it was like he was speaking Chinese.

In training, Harry would stop the game if someone made a square pass. He'd make you do press-ups if you passed it sideways. Kevin Richardson, a midfielder who had been at Everton and ended up going to Arsenal, wasn't going to agree with that.

## AGGRESSION

**David:** I was fearless, but I also knew that I wouldn't take any crap. I was quick, very quick, so often I'd end up marking the quicker of the two strikers. One player I remember was the Brazilian Mirandinha at Newcastle. We played them about five times one season and I relished the challenge of marking him. He couldn't run away from me so he didn't have the chance to do what he was good at.

I enjoyed marking people like Alan Shearer and Teddy Sheringham just as much. Shearer was a strong man. Against Blackburn once, I gave him plenty and he gave me one back, off the ball. I've had my nose broken 13 times, and three operations, so for me the physical side was part of the game. I put my head in where it hurts and I enjoyed leading by example. That's why I was captain.

We played at Millwall in the League Cup and I punched one of their players in the tunnel after the game. They had this idiot American kid [Bruce Murray] and he'd tried to do our goalkeeper, Simon Sheppard. He tried to kick him so I threw him in the goal and gave him a right-hook. Furs [Paul Furlong] had already been sent off for having a fight with their defender, Pat van den Hauwe.

As I walked off the pitch, this idiot American was bowing down to the Millwall fans, who were obviously giving me loads of abuse. I got back to the dressing room and Furs' eyes just lit up, like, 'Oh my God – what have you done?'

Then the idiot knocked on the dressing room door and said: 'Hey, man.'

I just smacked him and the stewards were barging in and there's more kerfuffle. It was a mad night, that, and I look back and think: 'Bloody hell – did I really do that?'

I say it now: every day there's a battle in your life and you've got to win it. It might just be having manners; it might just be turning up and being on time – punctuality and things like that. I'm strict with myself. Strict with my diet. I'm 45 and I'm in the best possible shape.

## GETTING INJURED

**Dean:** Away at Coventry, in the FA Youth Cup, I went in for a tackle, and someone's leg went straight across mine and took my knee out. I couldn't stand up – it was horrendous. I had no ligaments in my leg. I was told I would never play football, because at the time the operation had never been successful to get a player back from that. So they said to me: 'You've got to prepare for the worst.'

I went from scoring loads of goals in the youth team and being selected for the England under-18s, and then that happens, and all of a sudden your life has to re-adjust, very quickly. I was out for 11 months. Three operations and then lots of days climbing up and down the terraces with the physio on my back in the rain.

That was when people started judging us as twins. David was doing exceptionally well in the reserves, and I was the injured brother. There were a lot of tough days. Having been told I would never play again, part of me believed that until

I actually did play again. There were days when I was very
lonely, very upset. I spent seven weeks in plaster from top to
hip and I was on crutches. I had to go back after six months
and have the operation done again.

The pros at Watford – people like John Barnes and Luther
Blissett – were brilliant with me. I still see Luther and Barnesy
at golf days. I can be sitting there and John's giving me a
cuddle and he doesn't know that he's my hero. He used to pick
me up and take me to the ground so I didn't have to get the
bus. That's what team-mates do for each other.

**David:** Dean didn't have the same mentality as me. He just
wasn't strong-willed. He didn't have that in him, but when he
got his injury, he bulked up. He became physically stronger
and that was the best thing that could have happened to Dean.
He started to find some muscles. He wasn't an aggressive
person. I remember he was a good goalscorer but he was
lightweight. He had good mobility and was a good goalscorer,
but he wasn't physically strong. He spent a year in the weight
room and it made him stronger and a better player. He
became a bit more single-minded.

## STEVE HARRISON

**Dean:** Steve Harrison was the reserve team manager when I
was first at Watford and everyone knew him as 'Harry', but
he'd been away and then returned as manager.

I'll never work this out but the first day I saw him when he
came in as manager I said: 'Hello Harry.' He said: 'I'm "boss"
to you.'

'Wow,' I thought. Rather than saying: 'Listen, I'm going to
be known as boss now,' or, 'You need to call me boss from
now on,' he said that. I'd seen him as this great coach and a
great bloke, who I really respected.

When I was out on loan after my injury it was hurting him

that I was scoring goals. He'd sent a youngster out to score goals. I scored goals at Swansea, Port Vale and Brentford, came back and scored. By doing that, I was telling him I was better than what he'd got. That was hurting him, and I could see that, but it was the truth.

I knew there were clubs that wanted to sign me. Carlisle United had tried to sign me. Their manager, Clive Middlemass, tried to sign me for £35,000. I went to talk to Clive because I'd been on loan there but I was never, ever going to sign for Carlisle. It was five-and-a-half hours on the train, sitting outside a toilet with lager-swilling Jocks.

I said to Clive: 'I can't sign for you. My mum's away and she'd be distraught. She doesn't even know where Carlisle is.'

I got home and rang Steve Harrison and he berated me for 20 minutes for not joining Carlisle. He was saying I'd never play in the reserves again, never do this, never do that. I could have put the phone down on the side and come back to it ten minutes later and he'd still have been going.

In the end I said: 'I'll see you tomorrow for training. Whatever you want to do with me you can do with me but I don't want to be forced to go to Carlisle.' Then I put the phone down. Things changed massively after that.

I'd been to Port Vale on loan and I came back and played in a reserve game for Watford. We'd played okay, we'd worked hard, but Steve Harrison came in and questioned my attitude.

I'd had a pin in my knee, I had 82 stitches, I'd been out for a year, and I was training on my own every day, so I thought questioning my attitude was the last thing he could do.

It wasn't constructive, in my opinion, so I stood up and told him so. We came to... not quite nose-to-nose because he's got a bigger nose than me – but let's say we disagreed. But he was the manager, and he said to me: 'You'll go on the transfer list tomorrow.' And I said, 'Fine – no problem whatsoever. I'm really happy about that because I'm unhappy here.' And it was a shame, because I wanted to prove to Watford that I could do it in the first team.

Tom Walley rang me the night of the argument with Steve and I said: 'Tom, I can't play for someone who tells me that. I need to go and play football. I want to score goals.'

The next day I went to Brentford and signed a three-year contract. I'd been there on loan too so I knew the club.

**David:** When Harry questioned Dean, I was delighted to hear that he stood up for himself. That was the biggest thing for me. I remember once, years earlier, being at the park one day and we had jerseys down for goalposts. I had a shot and it's gone past Deano and this kid held the ball and said, 'No, take it off me.' So I'm standing there waiting. I said, 'Deano, get the ball.' The kid's really just taking the mickey out of him. So I just went over and smacked him. He wouldn't do it again. 'Deano, get the ball back next time – just hit him,' I said, And that was my mentality, because that's all I knew.

Later when he did that with Harry, it would have been a challenge for Dean because he wasn't really of that nature. But I was glad he stood up for himself after someone questioned his attitude after spending that long out. I got on great with Steve, but with Dean it was a different chemistry. We were twins but it doesn't make you the same.

**Dean:** Later, in my Premier League days, I did an article for a newspaper and I mentioned how I was treated by Steve and he sent me a letter. I've still got that letter.

He apologised for his behaviour and the way he treated me. He didn't realise how much of an effect it had had on me. It probably did me a bit of good and gave me a bit of burning fire in my belly, but it's a shame because he didn't need to be like that. All I wanted was to do well for him, so to be told my attitude was wrong was flabbergasting. I honestly felt it was because I was a Londoner and Steve was from the north. I still think that now.

## A SIXTH SENSE?

**David:** Dean and I have had this telepathy, if you like. It's amazing. He got rushed into hospital with appendicitis. The very next day, I went down in a heap with a burst appendix.

Deano smashed his right knee in, and his medial and his cruciate ligaments. I did my left, my lateral and my cruciate. I broke my left arm, he broke his right arm.

I went to play at Charlton and Dean told mum he felt weird. He said: 'I think David's got injured.' We didn't have mobile phones or anything so was just a sense. I came home that day on crutches.

**Dean:** We have definitely got a sixth sense. I know when he's wound-up as well. On the golf course I can wind him up because he gets so angry all the time.

We can be together and be really close or we can be apart and be very different. But we've never been 'in each other's pocket' close, you know? We could laugh about something together like no one else would laugh but we weren't always close.

**David:** We'll give each other a look, or a smile, or we'll laugh and we'll both start. I make no apologies for it because it's not intentional but we actually can be quite intimidating and it can be off-putting for people I suppose.

## DIFFERENCES

**Dean:** I was called 'the peacock' by people because I'd go into a room and my feathers would come up, so to speak. It was my ex-wife who said that and she was probably right. I think I did become like that.

Playing football and scoring goals gave me an edge. If the

ball came into the box, I knew I'd score. That confidence has probably been overpowering at some points – especially when I went to Wimbledon where we felt invincible.

It's a powerful place to be when you're a goalscorer, it really is. The mindset of a goalscorer is strong.

When I went to Wimbledon, I started modelling for Topman and I had my own range of clothes. I was invited to every party going. I wasn't ill-disciplined before a game and I was still totally dedicated in training but I probably thought I was invincible. I probably did become this powerful monster, you know – a bit of a big-head. I didn't treat people badly – I would never do that – but I think that was the beginning of the end of my relationship with my wife.

I became a single-minded person. In the dressing room at Wimbledon it was us against the world. We won at Manchester United twice. Once, we stood outside the dressing room at Old Trafford, with no clothes on, smoking cigars.

**David:** I got annoyed with Dean because he was becoming a different person. He became a real flash bastard and at Wimbledon he had this ego. They saw themselves as indestructible. Dean became a very different person. And football has that: money, goals, adulation, fans, women. All them things can change you.

I was happier sitting at the end of the bar; Dean would rather be standing on it. When you're around big characters you end up being one of those. Dean was around Fash [John Fashanu], Vinnie Jones and Joe Kinnear. They did like themselves. But Dean, credit where it's due, became a very good player. It changed him and I understand why.

I would never say I was boring, but I would never be out to be seen. I was very happy keeping out of that lifestyle. I wasn't worried about flash parties and worrying about who I was hanging around with.

But Dean enjoyed it and that became part of his world.

Dean was always the glamour boy and it didn't bother me. We'd to go to parties and I didn't want to be photographed. I didn't want to be in the paper. I was very happy keeping quiet. I remember going out with Miss Ireland and I just thought, 'What am I doing here?' Being in that position and thinking, 'I don't need this.' Once I went out, I was thinking, 'I can't do with this, I don't need people taking pictures of me.' Lovely looking girl, though.

I was proud to be captain of every club I've been at. I wanted people to understand that I wanted respect to be earned. A couple of senior players said, 'Your brother's a flash fucker,' and they were right but I would defend him still.

I only ever had one bit of trouble, in Sheffield, with a fan. A bloke was having a go at my brother. I said, 'Listen, you don't know my brother.' The bloke was drunk and he was having a go at me: 'Your brother's this and your brother's that.' I said, 'You don't even know my brother. What are you talking about?' A lot of fans have perceptions, don't they?

**Dean:** I have always wanted the best for him and I want the best for me. But you're always naturally compared as to who had the better career. People say to me, 'Oh, your brother did all right didn't he?' I go, 'My brother was a good player, he was a good centre-half.' He was tough – he was bloody hard.

## LOYALTY

**David:** Kevin Keegan at Newcastle came in for me and I had spoken to my agent, Jerome Anderson. I was in his office, and Jerome said to me: 'Kevin really likes you.'

I'd been playing well for Watford, I was in the England under-21s and I was loyal. I was loyal – that was it. I spoke to Kevin Keegan, he said, 'I want to buy you.' And I had no interest. They finished fifth from bottom the year before, and

nearly got relegated. And Newcastle's not around the corner. I
was happy, but do I look back with regret? No, I don't. I made
decisions for the right reasons. I was a loyal kid and I'm like
that now with
anybody. I was very loyal. It's not a negative in my opinion.
**Dean:** Personally, I think David should have left at some
point before and gone on. I know that Newcastle at the time
were very interested in him, and I think he should have gone
because he was doing really, really well. Looking at that career
path, he was loyal to Watford. Very loyal to Watford.

I think it was safe. He should have gone, he should have
taken that risk. That's probably where we are different. I think
you need to speculate to accumulate and have that risk, and
I always wonder: what if? I don't think that would come into
David's mind. If he'd gone to Newcastle or somewhere else
earlier, would it have been different?
**David:** I spent ten years playing at a high level for Watford
and I didn't get a testimonial. I would have liked to have
had one; I would have loved to have had one. I still believe
I should get one now. I believe that that loyalty should have
been repaid because there are not many players that stayed as
long as I did and saw the turmoil that I did.

When I left, I never even got a thank you. Never even got
a phone call. There had been talk of a move to Everton
previously but then I did my knee, and then there was a
chance for me to go to Crystal Palace. Steve Coppell had
made a bid but I was told and they wouldn't let me go because
it was a London club, which was mad.

They didn't want to offer me a new contract but they didn't
want me to go. In those days there was no Bosman ruling, by
the way, so it was a really precarious position.

All of a sudden, Kenny Jackett said: 'We've accepted a bid
from Sheffield United.' So I said, 'Well, okay. Howard

Kendall's the manager – I'll go up and talk to him.'

I hold it in my memory because I think I deserved more than that and I just felt the club should have shown some more class.

But I thought, 'If they don't want me, I'm going. If that loyalty is not going to be repaid I'm better off washing my hands – I'm going to go and play for a great manager and a big club like Sheffield United.'

It was a half-a-million pound deal and Watford did quite well out of it. I went to play for Howard Kendall – a great man, fantastic. Best manager I've ever worked for alongside Graham. They were very different types of people. I got on with Howard brilliantly and I would go and play for him on the moon.

Not to even get acknowledgement from Watford made me bitter. I'm not bitter about it now, it's gone, but I was for a couple of years. We beat Watford at Sheffield United 4-0 and I thought, 'You know what? I'm over the moon about that.' And I shouldn't have been that bitter then but it made me bitter because all I needed was a letter saying, 'David you've been a servant to us for a long time.' I didn't want a gold watch, all I wanted was a thanks, and I didn't get any.

It hurt my marriage at the time, because my ex-wife was from Essex. We had a very nice lifestyle but she hated being up north and it drove us apart. We had an ideal life, we were comfortable and we had children who went to school 25 minutes away.

It just made me realise that footballers are a piece of meat. It shouldn't have been that way. They should have sent me just a thanks.

But when I went back to Watford, I got a great reception from the fans, which was lovely. I got introduced onto the pitch and I hold that in my heart.

## PLAYING TOGETHER

**David:** I was quicker. Don't get me wrong – he was a good player, but I came out on top in those battles, without a doubt.

**Dean:** I scored two goals against Sheffield United and he never spoke to me for a month. The problem is that when you play against each other, the rivalry is so high. If I don't score, he's then had the best game, hasn't he? So it's not enjoyable.

When we used to train against each other, we used to kick lumps out of each other. Tom Walley would often tear us apart. I wouldn't say it was enjoyable, but we were trying to be better than the other person, so it drove us forward.

## MANAGEMENT

**Dean:** When I was manager of Newport, we played his team, Mansfield. That week I trained the team for one reason. We were working to get one corner, one moment in the game that made all the difference. We didn't get a corner in the first half. I said to the team: 'Don't worry about it – we're going to get a corner at some point.' I think it was the 64th minute, and all my players had a signal: the fingers. Charlie Henry took the corner. Danny Rose looked at me, nodded, and ran back towards the halfway line and started doing up his laces. Then he made his run and arrived at the edge of the box, met the ball and smashed it straight in the top corner. The roof came off at Newport. The TV cameras were there and David's reaction is brilliant. He smashes his water bottle on the floor because he didn't want to lose.

**David:** It was bloody lucky. We had three cleared off the line – Christ Almighty. He had a million-pound budget and I had 50 pence. Newport were good people and he did really well there, but he doesn't talk about the pre-season game we won 3-0. He banked on this corner and he got lucky, but we were the better team and played the better football.

## BETTER RELATIONSHIP

**David:** We've both got an edge to us and we fall out because of that. We're both strong-willed. Can I be a better brother? I think we all can be better people. How could I be a better brother? By stopping him eating too many burgers.

**Dean:** Would I have been a better brother by not scoring two against Sheffield United, or not scoring the penalty against Birmingham? Without getting too personal, there are times where we both could have done with living closer together.

**David:** We were thick as thieves as kids and everyone knew we'd be together. We would be compared to the Krays when we were kids, which was hilarious, really. If Dean was in trouble, Christ, I'd be the first one there. Without a doubt. And we know that about each other.

## WHO IS THE BETTER FOOTBALLER?

**Dean:** Me. I was flamboyant, you know. I wouldn't want to watch a centre-half kick people all day and stamp on people. David was just a hard-nosed centre-half. He couldn't tell me about flair, could he? I'll always say it's me because I scored goals every time I played against him.

**David:** Me, because he was just a goalscorer. I could do more than that. We both had good careers, long careers. We both had ups and downs.

I would say I was a seven or eight out of ten each week. He'd either be a ten or a four. But, you know, fans don't give a monkeys about centre-halves. I was just a boring sod, but I think it's nice to be known as reliable and strong.

I played in a charity game the other week and I still take it so seriously. Howard Webb refereed it and I clipped this guy and he said, 'You won't change, will you?'

I'm 45 and I still take it too seriously – far too seriously. But I think that's what makes me the person I am.

# TOMMY SMITH

**On returning to Watford**
'It felt like a big decision because, although I loved the club, I wasn't sure how the fans would react because of how I had left. I felt like it gave me an opportunity to go back and do well.'

# 10

For all the talk about the potential of young players, the statistics show that a fraction of them make it in the professional game.

Fewer still go on to play hundreds of games for their local club.

Tommy Smith is one of those few. In two spells with the Hornets he made himself a genuine hero with his committed and energetic style of play.

Now, as the end of his career approaches, he looks back on what Watford means to him.

# TOMMY SMITH

If, like me, you spent your childhood dreaming of becoming a professional footballer, you can probably pinpoint the moment you realised it wasn't going to come true. My uncomfortable collision with reality came during my first week at secondary school.

We gathered on the top playing field and the PE teacher read out every boy's name and asked what position they preferred to play. 'Right midfield,' I said, slightly frustrated that the teacher had moved on to the next boy before I'd had a chance to add that I liked to cut inside but was equally comfortable dropping deep to cover for an overlapping full-back. The teacher then divided us into teams and we played several games on the school's large playing field, watched – assessed – by the PE staff. The pressure... Goodness me, the pressure.

At morning break the following day, two team line-ups had been posted on the noticeboard outside the changing rooms. My eyes went straight for the right-midfield spot in the first eleven. There must have been some mistake, I thought, because my name was not there. Instead, I was in the same position for the 'B' team. The sense of crushing disappointment was not helped by the fact I had double maths coming up.

That day, only a couple of months past my 11th birthday, I knew I would not make it as a professional footballer. If I couldn't get into the Hemel Hempstead School first year 'A' team, I was unlikely to catch the eye of any Watford scouts.

* * *

Five years later, Tommy Smith went through the same ritual at the same school. I was vaguely aware that the school had a couple of talented players in the lower years – Mark Bircham, who went on to play for Queens Park Rangers, was a couple of years below me – and I imagined that their brilliance must have been obvious from a very early age.

So, when I meet Tommy Smith in Berkhamsted after he'd finished a day's training with Brentford, I'm surprised to hear that he'd not been head and shoulders above every other boy in his year group.

'I used to infuriate my dad, I think, because I had quite a lot of talent but I was always on the periphery of things,' he says. 'I used to stand out wide and I'd chew holes in my sleeves, which used to drive my mum mad too. Dad said that when I got the ball I was great but then I wouldn't touch it again for ten minutes.

'Confidence was a big thing for me. When I was younger I was quite little, quite timid. By secondary school I was beginning to come into my own a bit more.'

He must have been quite good because his dad spoke to Hemel Hempstead School's head of PE, Graham Cracknell, and ensured young Tommy got a place at the school despite being on the boundary of the catchment area. 'My dad had been to school with Mr Cracknell and so they spoke and he suggested I might be a good addition to the school,' he says. 'We were quite a strong year group. Three or four of us trained with pro clubs but I wouldn't say I was the outstanding one. I was on a par with that group.'

Smith's dad, David, had been on the cusp of a career in football, until his father intervened. 'I'm a bit sketchy on the details,' says Smith. 'My dad doesn't live in the past at all, so it's hard getting stories out of him but I know he played for Watford reserves. But his dad wanted him to do his A-Levels, so he told Watford he didn't want his son playing for them. It was a completely different world then; there wasn't the money in the game. But having said that, my dad says he has never regretted the decision.'

Football was Smith's life from a very early age. 'My earliest memories are of me and my brother, who is three-and-a-half years younger than me, playing football,' he says. Jack Smith also played for Watford before moving to Swindon and on again to Millwall.

'Football is all we did. We had a couple of goals in the back garden and we played until it was dark. Then we got up in the morning and went back out there and played all day. I played for the cubs and for Hemel Comets, who used to play in a set of old QPR kit – blue and white hoops.'

If they weren't playing football, they were watching it, although their loyalties were split. 'My dad was from the north east – he moved down with his family when he was about ten – so his side of the family were all massive Newcastle fans,' says Smith. 'My mum was from Abbots Langley and her family supported Watford. So I watched both teams, although we saw a lot more of Watford. My dad took us to see Newcastle when they were playing in the south. This was the early 1990s when Kevin Keegan came back. We saw quite a lot of games and it was great fun.'

* * *

The first time Watford fans might have heard the name Tommy Smith was during the 1996-97 season when the youth team reached the fifth round of the FA Youth Cup, knocking out Manchester United on the way. After drawing 1-1 at Old

Trafford – with man-child Gifton Noel-Williams leading the line – Tommy Smith gave Watford an early lead in the replay at Vicarage Road, which turned into a ding-dong cup tie played without fear. United scored twice early in the second half before Andy Johnson converted a penalty and his twin brother Chris blasted home a late winner to send the Hornets through to meet Luton Town.

A look at the team that played in the replay against Manchester United shows how the odds are stacked against every young player when it comes to making it in the professional game: Rogers, Boyce, Cave, C Johnson, Pluck, Panayi, Smith, Grieves, Cornock, A Johnson, Perpetuini.

Smith was one of only six to play for the first team. Of them, Chris Johnson and Colin Pluck (who changed his surname to Miles for family reasons in 2004) played just once for Watford's first team. Daniel Grieves, the great grandson of Skilly Williams, the legendary Watford goalkeeper from the 1910s and 1920s, also played once, but in an Auto Windscreens Shield cup tie that featured eight reserve players and a trialist. James Panayi played 13 games for Watford before moving to play in Cyprus and David Perpetuini made 18 appearances, including some in the Premiership, and made a good career for himself at Gillingham. The Johnson twins, Andy and Chris, looked set to make it as professionals – until they fell foul of Graham Taylor's strict rules regarding young players, curfews and night-clubs, and were sacked.

That puts Tommy Smith's achievements into context. His career has spanned 19 seasons, and taken him to seven different clubs, including two spells at Watford under six different managers. He has played almost 500 games, scoring almost 100 goals. He's been bought and sold for more than £2.6million, won the Championship title with two separate clubs – Queens Park Rangers and Portsmouth – and was voted Watford's player of the season two years running. He is 14th on Watford's all-time list of top league scorers, although he will probably have been overtaken by Troy Deeney by the time you read this.

But back in the spring of 1997, having just scored against Manchester United's youth team, Smith had no inkling that he would make it further than the others. 'It was drilled into us that we had to do our jobs around the club: clean the boots, work hard on the training pitch and keep our heads down,' he says. 'I thought at the time we'd all make it. I thought we were all good players. I really don't know what separates one player from another although I had a burning desire to be the best. I would listen to everything and take absolutely anything that a coach said to me on board. I had some great coaches when I was young. Rob Kelly was the youth team manager the season we beat Manchester United. He was a great man and when he left at the end of that season, to go to Blackburn, I was really disappointed. He's the assistant manager at West Brom now, which doesn't surprise me at all.

'I also had Kenny Jackett and I thought his coaching was brilliant. He was a tough, tough man. He would not take anything less than 100 per cent from everybody, every day. He was on you relentlessly if you dropped off just a tiny bit. He would ring on a Friday night and when the phone went at nine o'clock I'd say to mum, "Don't worry, I'll get it. That'll be Ken." When I moved up to the reserve team, Tom Walley was the manager for a while so I moved from one tough man to some-one who was even tougher. It was a great education.

'But there was never any chance to get carried away. Beating Manchester United was the best thing I'd achieved at the time but it didn't change anything. I remember we lost to Luton on penalties in the next round. We'd drawn against them twice but, really, we'd murdered them twice and then lost.'

The following season, Smith got his first taste of first-team action. 'It was a home game against Oldham and I came on for Ronny Rosenthal,' he says. 'I remember that vividly, shaking his hand as he came off and I went on. Ronny was such a big name to have at the club so to come on for him was a really good feeling.'

However, it would be more than a year before Smith got another significant chance. At Loftus Road, Smith entered the fray as a 69th-minute substitute. Within 60 seconds, he'd put the ball in the back of the net, scoring the winner against Queens Park Rangers.

'I was on the fringes of the first-team more during that season in the First Division,' he says. 'That day at QPR is all a bit of a blur and I think it always will be. I scored with my first touch. I went on the pitch, the cross came in and somehow I bundled it into the corner.'

That goal secured three crucial points in the race to reach the play-offs and although Smith did not figure much during that amazing run-in, he felt part of the excitement. 'I loved every minute of it,' he says. 'I was 18 so just to be involved and training with the team was fantastic. I sat on the bench at Wembley with my club suit on. What an experience that was. In a way, it was the best possible experience. I wasn't nervous because I knew I wasn't playing, so I could enjoy it. Being on the team bus, seeing the fans on Wembley Way, was unforget-table. I'd scored a couple of goals – the one against QPR and I got another one against Ipswich – so I felt like I'd contributed. Graham Taylor was brilliant at reminding you that you'd played a part.'

Promotion meant that Smith, still only 19, continued his footballing education in the Premiership. It was a place where he found he had to learn quickly. 'The Premiership was ruth-less,' he says. 'When I compare it to the Premier League now, I think it was even tougher back then because the divide between the Premiership and the First Division was much bigger. Even the teams that were average in the Premiership had three or four really top-class players.

Graham Taylor was never scared of giving young players an opportunity and so Smith was thrown in regardless of the opposition. He was on the bench for the league game at Manchester United, which Watford eventually lost 4-1, and watched as their imposing centre half, Jaap Stam, went off injured. 'I was thinking, "Yes, this is brilliant – I might get a chance," because Stam was a colossus but then they dropped Roy Keane in at the back and it couldn't have got any worse! I went on and I was clean through against the keeper, Mark Bosnich, and should have scored.'

Creating chances and scoring goals can be hard work against the top defences and Smith played alongside several different types of forward during the Premiership season. There was the enthusiasm and never-say-die spirit of Tommy Mooney, the controlled aggression of Heidar Helguson and the *je ne sais quoi* of Xavier Gravelaine.

'He was an enigma,' Smith says of the Frenchman. 'He was a strange guy. I could see why he was brought in because he did have some ability. But the Premier League was so physical I think it was a real eye-opener for him. Football in other countries was nowhere near as physical then. It was very hard away from home because we couldn't afford to carry him.'

Helguson, on the other hand, gave everything in every match, although his ability was not always apparent in training. Smith has subsequently played with the Icelandic striker at Queens Park Rangers and Cardiff, and he has never changed. 'He was a terrible trainer,' says Smith. 'He'd do something in training and I'd think, "What have you seen there?" But when he got on the pitch for a first-team game he was a completely different player. He is the kind of guy who will run through a brick wall for you and I wonder if he needs to sort of hold something back in training so that he can channel all of that energy into his games.'

\* \* \*

Following relegation, Watford enjoyed a terrific start to the season and scored seemingly at will. They had so many options when it came to forward players. Gifton Noel-Williams was fit again having missed much of the previous 18 months through injury. Tommy Mooney was also firing on all cylinders having been ruled out of large chunks of the Premiership campaign. Helguson and Smith were also in great form.

'GT played me wide, which I really enjoyed because it gave me more freedom,' Smith says. 'We had Gifton, Heidar and Tommy to aim for in the middle – three players who would get on the end of anything if you put it in the right areas. It was the first time I felt like I was more or less an automatic selection and that gives a player a lot of confidence. We were flying. It was great to be back alongside Gifton up front, too. We'd been playing together since we were 13 and he always looked after me on the pitch. If someone clattered me, he'd get them back for me! We'd grown up together – although having said that, he'd grown up quicker than me because he had about three kids by the time he was 21."

Like Micah Hyde, Smith is unable to explain what went wrong as the runaway train that seemed destined for promotion ran off the tracks. 'I was too young to really know why it happened,' he says. 'I was just trying my best but I didn't have the experience to fall back on when things started to get really tough. I was still trying my hardest to do well but it wasn't working and we didn't know how to get it going again. It's an incredibly hard league, the Championship, as it is now. People underestimate how tough it is – 46 games and everyone can beat everyone else on their day. If the top team drops off a little bit they can lose to a team at the bottom, no problem. It was my first full season and it turned into a long, long, hard season. Graham brought in one or two players to try to jump-start us – I remember Carlton Palmer came in – but it didn't really work, did it?

Gianluca Vialli's arrival excited and energised Smith but the Italian's decision to hand him the number nine shirt when he allocated the squad numbers raised expectations. Vialli referred to Smith by a nickname, Smudger, and called him the team's 'fox in the box'. Although Smith says he loved all that, it perhaps wasn't the best use of his talents because he was never prolific – 17 was his biggest tally in a Watford shirt, in 2008-09.

'Working with Vialli was great,' says Smith. 'He showed me a different side of the game but he wanted us to play total football. He wanted us to pass it, pass it. There was a lot of side-ways passing and I'd be making these runs and the ball would never arrive. I'd run into one channel, then back into the other channel, making big arcing runs and I wouldn't touch the ball for five minutes. I think we overdid that a bit.'

Vialli had signed Marcus Gayle from Glasgow Rangers for £900,000 just before the season began. Gayle had been a success at Wimbledon, but as a winger. Watford now found themselves with two strikers who would both have been more comfortable causing havoc coming in from wider positions.

'I think Vialli was looking for that big man, little man thing. Everyone was looking for their version of Niall Quinn and Kevin Phillips at Sunderland. In theory it was a good idea but the crowd got frustrated and I got frustrated doing all that running for nothing. There was a gradual realisation that it wasn't the right way to play in that league – there were teams that we just weren't hurting with that style of play.'

* * *

Another season, another manager – Ray Lewington – and another strike partner in Danny Webber. A good FA Cup run alleviated the club's financial problems following the collapse of ITV Digital and the Vialli experiment. The players had agreed to defer part of their wages and one of the conditions was that if they earned extra money from a cup run the players would be repaid from that. 'That tells you something about footballers,' Smith jokes. 'We reached the semi-final.'

But the experience did not turn out to be a happy one for Smith. He had scored a twice-taken penalty at the Stadium of Light against Sunderland in the FA Cup fifth round. 'I didn't hit it well,' he says, with a shake of the head. 'The keeper guessed right and it was a nice height for him. So I was relieved that the ref ordered it to be retaken. Someone came up to me – I don't remember who – and said that they'd take the second kick but I said, "No way – I've got to finish this." I didn't hit the second one much better – the keeper got a hand on it – but it went in.'

Smith scored again in the 2-0 quarter-final win over Burnley but it was another match against the Clarets that turned the course of his season and, indeed, his career. In a league match at Turf Moor shortly before Watford were due to face Southampton in the FA Cup semi-final, on-loan striker Michael Chopra scored four times in an extraordinary 7-4 win.

The manager, Ray Lewington, explains in his chapter in this book the thought process that led to him putting Chopra in the team for the Villa Park match, leaving Smith to take a place on the bench.

For Smith's part, it was a decision that more or less opened the door for him to leave Watford. 'I had scored against Burnley to get us into the semi-final and then he left me out. I was livid. I was absolutely livid. Really, really angry,' he adds, for emphasis.

It's clear it still stings. 'I went into his office and said, "How the hell can you leave me out?" It was the first time anything like this had happened to me but you can see it with most managers – they are not going to change their minds. He wasn't going to agree with me, so I just had to take it but yes, I was angry about that for a long time.

'It changed things with the manager – certainly it did for me. To get left out of a cup semi-final for a guy who's on loan, it's bound to. I know Chopra had scored four goals but I still thought it was the wrong decision. It was a tough, tough day because I felt I should be playing.'

Smith came on – for Chopra – after 70 minutes with the Hornets still in it at 1-0 down. But Southampton scored again ten minutes from the end, although Gayle pulled one back in the dying minutes.

The disappointment of not making it to Wembley was one thing, but Smith already knew he was going to have to leave Watford – the club he'd been at for ten years.

'Things were hard after that and I think it helped me make the decision to go,' he says. 'I felt the club and I were going in different directions. I needed to push on and go somewhere else and I felt Watford were sort of getting further away from pushing for the play-offs.'

Watford did offer Smith a contract but Smith says: 'I felt Watford were playing the game a little bit. It wasn't a very good contract and it was over three years but I think they were saying to the fans, "Well, we've offered him a contract." That's how football is. The thing is, I don't think I'd have stayed at that time no matter what they offered me.'

Smith's relationship with Lewington did not repair before he left the club. 'I was still mad about it,' he says. 'I've bumped into him since and it's fine. It's a long time ago now and if I saw him now it would be okay but at the time, yeah, it hurt.'

Smith signed for Sunderland in the summer of 2003 and played his part as the Black Cats reached the play-offs, although they lost in the semi-finals. After just one year, he moved on to Derby County and the Rams also lost out in the play-offs. Having spent his whole career with a club that was on his doorstep, Smith enjoyed the experience of playing away from home. 'I loved it at Sunderland,' he says. 'It's such a massive club but, although the spotlight was always on you, I found that I could get away from football a bit after games. When I played for Watford, often my family and friends would be at games and people would say, "Why did you miss that chance?" It can be hard at first, and it can be annoying at times, because on a Saturday evening you want to forget about it a bit. You see your family for Sunday lunch and they want to talk about the game, so it kind of broke that routine for a while. It was the same at Derby and I enjoyed the experience at both clubs.'

In August 2006, Smith had the chance to return to Watford, who had bludgeoned their way into the Premier League under Aidy Boothroyd. The season was already under way but as the clock ticked towards the transfer deadline, it seemed increasingly likely that Smith would be returning home, for £500,000.

'I'd been in protracted talks with Neil Warnock at Sheffield United,' he says. 'Derby were trying to sort it out but then Watford came in with a late bid. It felt like a big decision because, although I loved the club, I wasn't sure how the fans would react because of how I had left. I felt like it gave me an opportunity to go back and do well. I felt I had become a better player. I'd lived away for three years, we'd had a daughter and so my life had changed.'

Watford had also changed. 'It was unrecognisable,' he says. 'Aidy had made so many changes to the staff – it was a completely different club, so it was a bit alien to start with. It didn't take long – I knew very early on that I'd made the right decision.

'I loved Aidy. He was one of my biggest influences, off the pitch. I was older [Smith was 26 when he came back] and was becoming a bit more of a leader in the dressing room. He expected us to talk openly about how we felt. The mentality was that we were all big men and that we could say what we felt about other players and take it on the chin when people told us what they thought of us. He believed that was how we'd get better.

'I'd never been under a manager who wanted us to do that. To start with it was horrible, really nerve-wracking. We'd sit there after every game and we'd have to talk openly. If I had played right-midfield, Aidy would ask me to say how I thought the right-back had done. Aidy would ask what the right-back had done well and what he'd done badly and he wouldn't let you get away with saying nothing. He'd say, "What, so he had the perfect game, did he?" It wasn't about point-scoring or criticising your team-mates, it was about suggesting what others could do to get better. And then he'd ask someone how they thought I'd done and I'd have to sit there and listen. I'd never experienced it before but I quite enjoyed it.'

Watford struggled at times but Smith felt they acquitted themselves well. 'I thought we did okay. Losing Marlon King didn't help, although that's not an excuse. When you are fighting to stay up you need things to go your way. We were close to getting things right but we lacked a bit of quality and a bit of luck but we weren't too far off.'

The lowest point was probably the 1-0 defeat to Sheffield United at Vicarage Road on a Tuesday night at the end of November. That was a match Watford needed to win. Neither side covered themselves in glory. 'I remember thinking, "This is turgid." At one point I was talking to their left back and said, "Dear me, this is dreadful." I felt for the fans that night because it was a poor game but it was one of those matches that neither team could afford to lose. The nerves took over and we cancelled each other out in everything we did.'

Although relegation was on the cards by mid-April, the season was brightened by another run to the FA Cup semi-final, where they faced Manchester United at Villa Park. This time, Smith played, although the Hornets lost 4-1.

There was another case of *déja-vu* the following season when they got out of the blocks very quickly, built up a nice lead at the top of the table and looked set to mount a serious pro-motion challenge, just as they had in 2000 after their previous relegation from the Premiership.

Boothroyd's team had reacted in the same way to Taylor's side six years earlier and Smith certainly saw similarities in the two managers. 'They are both very charismatic men who are big characters,' he says. 'They are very good at getting the best out of players and at building confidence. Aidy had us walking across hot coals for a bit of a team bonding exercise. They had similar styles of football and I fitted in well because I liked crossing to big guys in the box.'

The way Watford fell away so dramatically, just as they had before, was astonishing and Smith feels he has some answers as to why it happened the second time around. 'I think it was simply that teams worked us out,' he says. 'We blew teams away at the start but after a couple of months they'd had a chance to watch us. We were a bit one-dimensional with our style. We didn't have a Plan B and teams came to Vicarage Road, sat back and said, "Okay, break us down." And we couldn't do it. It's such a different game when teams come and sit deep and say, "Go on, beat us." They let us have the ball. They singled out players they were happy to let have the ball and we couldn't break them down. It was massively frustrating because we had started so well.'

Watford slipped down the table but clung on to the final play-off slot on goal difference. Just before the first leg of the play-off semi-final, against Hull City at Vicarage Road, Boothroyd had a surprise in store.

'The Thursday before the game, he said we were going to change our formation. He said, "We're going to play football. I want you to express yourselves. I don't want any long ball. I want you to pass it." I thought we played quite well and were a bit unlucky but we lost 2-0. Then we went away from home, scored the early goal and I thought we were going to do it. Their crowd went quiet and were moaning a bit. Then there was a bit of a mistake for their equaliser and we capitulated.' The final score was 4-1 to Hull.

The start of the following season continued the downward trend. In November, Boothroyd was sacked. 'At the time I was surprised Aidy went but I think you're so close to it you don't really see it,' Smith says. 'We lost at home to Blackpool and the performances were getting worse, not better. I always thought we'd bounce back but on reflection it wasn't going to improve and I think the powers that be could see that.'

Perhaps the departure of Boothroyd's experienced right-hand man Keith Burkinshaw hastened his demise. 'I think Aidy relied on Keith a lot,' says Smith. 'Keith was his eyes and ears and he would watch every training session, he'd watch the reserves and the under-21s. He'd sit in the stand to get a different perspective. They were very different – a bit of an odd fit in a way – but it worked. Keith challenged Aidy possibly at a time when no one else could. Sometimes Keith would suggest an idea in a meeting and Aidy would say, "Really? No, Keith, we're not going to do that."'

The players were convinced Malky Mackay would be

Boothroyd's replacement, particularly after they defeated Queens Park Rangers 3-0 while the Scot was in charge as caretaker manager.

'There were two people in for the job: Malky, who had been coaching us, and this other guy who nobody had ever heard of,' says Smith. 'Why would you employ a guy who no one has ever heard of and who has no experience? There was no way he was going to get it.'

But Brendan Rodgers did get the job and he had to walk into the Watford dressing room and establish himself as the boss. 'He couldn't have been more different to Aidy,' says Smith. 'He was quieter but he chatted more to you one-to-one. Aidy was the boss, the leader and the man in charge. He could be friendly but when you were at work, you were at work. Brendan was a lot chattier around the club. Training was different. It was a lot more football-based: we got the ball on the floor and did a lot of small, intensive sessions.

'He wanted us to play total football. He wanted to play 5-3-2 and pass it but it didn't work to start with so he had to be more pragmatic and adapt it. We went to a back four. I think he'd have liked to have stuck to the purest style possible but he adapted it to get us out of trouble and we ended up comfortable in mid-table.

'I'd really enjoyed the second half of the season. I loved working with Brendan, and I felt we'd grown as a team. I was so confident we could push for the play-offs so when he rang me while I was on holiday to tell me he was leaving [to join Reading] I was disappointed.

'I am not surprised he's done so well since. I was not in the least bit surprised he nearly won the league with Liverpool. He was a very good coach.'

It would not be long before Smith followed Rodgers through the exit door. He had been player of the season and had scored

17 league goals, making him one of the Hornets' most saleable assets.

'It was another deadline-day move,' he says. 'The Russos said that the club needed to recoup some money and that two or three of us needed to be sold. So Mike Williamson and I were sold to Portsmouth because Watford couldn't really afford to keep us.

'I didn't really want to leave but I did feel that the club wasn't moving in the right direction. They were tightening the purse strings and seemed to be happy being a mid-table team in the Championship. I felt that for my career it was probably best for me to move on.'

Smith scored in his final game in a Watford shirt, in a 2-2 draw against Blackpool, although that was not his last goal at Vicarage Road.

He returned with Queens Park Rangers in April 2011 and scored the last-minute goal that confirmed the Championship title for the west London side. Although most Watford fans were not too enamoured with the Rangers fans that day, it speaks volumes for his popularity that no one begrudged Smith his moment.

'Watford is such a huge chunk of who I am,' he says. 'I was there from the age of 13 to 23. It made me the man I am now.'

After travelling to Portsmouth and Cardiff, Smith took the decision for his young family to move to Brentford so he could be at home. He doesn't want his children moving schools – or changing football teams, for that matter.

'It's the first time in my career that I said to my agent, "Here's a radius from my home. I don't want to go any further than that."'

Smith says he doesn't fancy football management or coaching – certainly not in the immediate future. He's happy coaching his son's Berko Raiders under-eights team. 'Friends of mine who are a similar age to me are getting started in coaching and management,' he says. 'I would never say never but it's like extending your playing career. You have to be prepared to move with the job. It's very stressful. It's not something I want to do at the moment.'

For now, the priority is to ensure that the next generation of Smiths make the correct decision when it comes to the most important issue of all: who to support.

'My son is seven now and he's a bit confused because he's been a Portsmouth fan, a Cardiff fan and a QPR fan. But we bought him a Watford shirt for his birthday in the summer so I'm pushing to make sure he's a Watford fan.'